J. I. PACKER

FOREWORD BY MARK DEVER

EVANGELISM AND THE SOVEREIGNTY OF GOD

IVP Books

An imprint of InterVarsity Press
Downers Grove, Illinois

InterVarsity Press
P.O. Box 1400, Downers Grove, IL 60515-1426
World Wide Web: www.ivpress.com
E-mail: email@ivpress.com

InterVarsity Press® is the book-publishing division of InterVarsity Christian Fellowship/USA®, a student movement active on campus at hundreds of universities, colleges and schools of nursing in the United States of America, and a member movement of the International Fellowship of Evangelical Students. For information about local and regional activities, write Public Relations Dept., InterVarsity Christian Fellowship/USA, 6400 Schroeder Rd., P.O. Box 7895, Madison, WI 53707-7895, or visit the IVCF website at <www.intervarsity.org>.

Cover design: Cindy Kiple
Interior design: Beth Hagenberg
Images: Lonny Kalfus/Getty Images

ISBN 978-0-8308-3799-1

Printed in the United States of America ∞

Library of Congress Cataloging-in-Publication Data

Packer, J. I. (James Innell)
 Evangelism & the sovereignty of God / J. I. Packer.
  p. cm.
 Originally published: Evangelism and the sovereignty of God. 1961.
With new foreword.
 Includes bibliographical references.
 ISBN 978-0-8308-3799-1 (pbk.: alk. paper)
 1. Evangelistic work. 2. Providence and government of God. I.
Title. II. Title: Evangelism and the sovereignty of God.
 BV3793.P3 2012
 231.7—dc23

2011047309

P	17	16	15	14	13	12	11	10	9	8	7	6		
Y	26	25	24	23	22	21	20	19	18	17	16	15		

CONTENTS

FOREWORD

Before J. I. Packer became an evangelical superstar with the publication of *Knowing God* in 1973, he had already made important contributions to evangelical readers. Packer had a knack for addressing key topics succinctly and powerfully. What others would do in long and ponderous tomes, Packer would address, fairly and squarely, with a little volume of three or four chapters. The clarion call for "God-centeredness," long before John Piper's *Desiring God* or even Packer's own *Knowing God,* was Packer's little introduction for the republication of John Owen's *The Death of Death in the Death of Christ.* The loss of faith in Scripture he met with the little volume *"Fundamentalism" and the Word of God.* And, in July of 1961 appeared the book you now hold in your hands—*Evangelism and the Sovereignty of God.*

The title both summarizes the content and invites the reader perfectly. Various people are called to read the book by this simple title. Are you interested in evangelism? This book will address it directly by explaining what it is, and the need for it, in terms that are both simple and theologically careful. It will help you evangelize better.

Are you interested in the doctrine of God's sovereignty? This book is for you. In the most basic yet informed way, Packer addresses the simple question, "If God is in control, why should we do anything at all? Why should we work? Why should we pray? And especially, why should we evangelize?"

Packer addresses this question so clearly and biblically that this book is good for anyone who is beginning to wrestle with questions of how God's sovereignty can fit with any area of human responsibility. I've often recommended this book to faithful Christians who are confused about how they are to think about prayer, missions, giving—any area in which our efforts could be wrongly pitted against God's own necessary action. Packer introduces us to clear truths, handles Scripture with exemplary care, and supplies us with just the right amount of illustrations and application.

In this book, an antinomy is helpfully distinguished from a paradox. Opposites are explained. Cheap theological points are never scored. Packer insists that divine sovereignty and human responsibility are doctrines that need no reconciling. Instead, they are, as Packer calls them, "friends."

Throughout this volume, agreement is graciously assumed as Packer leads us to lay aside old divisions and, again, consider together the Bible, and the Bible's God. Though written almost fifty years ago, this book is timeless. *Evangelism and the Sovereignty of God* was written out of a warm Christian experience, and it assumes the reader is reading out of that same affection for God. In this book, speculation fades and trust increases. And as that happens, we find ourselves becoming more faithful—and more frequent!—evangelists.

If you would like to share in that experience, do what so many other readers have done, what I have done, what many I've given this book to over the years have done: pray, and read on.

Mark Dever
Senior Pastor, Capitol Hill Baptist Church, Washington, D.C.

PREFACE

The nucleus of the following discourse was an address given at the Pre-Mission Conference of the London Inter-Faculty Christian Union on October 24, 1959. It has been expanded in the hope of giving it a wider usefulness. Its origin, and the practical nature of its subject matter, accounts for its homiletical style.

Lest its purpose be misconceived, may I say at the outset what it is not.

It is not a blueprint for evangelistic action today, though it sets out relevant principles for determining any evangelistic strategy.

It is not a contribution to the current controversy about modern evangelistic methods, though it lays down relevant principles for settling that controversy.

It is not a critique of the evangelistic principles of any particular person or persons, though it provides relevant principles for evaluating all evangelistic activities.

What is it, then? It is a piece of biblical and theological reasoning, designed to clarify the relationship between three realities: God's sovereignty, man's responsibility and the Christian's evangelistic duty. The last of these is its proper subject; divine sovereignty and human responsibility are discussed only so far as they bear on evangelism. The aim of the discourse is to dispel the suspicion (current, it seems, in some quarters) that faith in the absolute sovereignty of God hinders a full recognition and acceptance of evangelistic responsibility, and to show that, on the contrary, only this faith can give Christians the strength that they need to fulfill their evangelistic task.

It must not be thought that on all the points with which I deal I am trying to lay down some sort of "I.V.F. orthodoxy." The limits of "I.V.F. orthodoxy" are set out in the Fellowship's doctrinal basis. Beyond those limits, members of the Fellowship are free, in John Wesley's phrase, to "think and let think," and no opinion on any subject can be regarded as the only one permissible. On the subject now to be dealt with, it may well be that some members of the Fellowship will think differently from the present writer. Equally, however, an author has a right to his own opinion, and he cannot be expected to conceal his views when he believes them to be biblical, relevant and (in the strict sense) edifying.

J. I. Packer

INTRODUCTION

Always and everywhere the servants of Christ are under orders to evangelize, and I hope that what I shall say now will act as an incentive to this task. I hope, too, that it will serve a further purpose. There is in Christian circles at the present time much heart-searching and dispute about ways and means of evangelism. I want to speak about the spiritual factors involved in evangelizing, and I hope that what I say may help toward resolving some of the current disagreements and debates.

Evangelism is my proper subject, and I am to speak of it in relation to the sovereignty of God. That means that I shall not be speaking of the sovereignty of God further than is necessary for right thinking about evangelism. Divine sovereignty is a vast subject: it embraces everything that comes into the biblical picture of God as Lord and King in his world, the One who "works all things according to the counsel of his will," (Eph 1:11), directing every process and ordering every event for the fulfilling of his own eternal plan. To deal with such a subject in full, one would have to take soundings in the depths, not merely of providence, but also of predestination and the last things, and that is more than we can or need do here. The only aspect of divine sovereignty that will concern us in these pages is God's sovereignty in grace: his almighty action in bringing helpless sinners home through Christ to himself.

In examining the relationship between God's sovereignty and the Christian's task of evangelism, I have a specific aim in view. There is abroad today a widespread suspicion that a robust faith in the absolute sovereignty of God is bound to undermine any adequate sense of human responsibility. Such a faith is thought to be dangerous to spiritual health, because it breeds a habit of complacent inertia. In particular, it is thought to paralyze evangelism by robbing one both of the motive to evangelize and of the message to evangelize with. The supposition seems to be that you cannot evangelize effectively unless you are prepared to pretend while you are doing it that the doctrine of divine sovereignty is not true. I shall try to make it evident that this is nonsense. I shall try to show further that, so far from inhibiting evangelism, faith in the sovereignty of God's government and grace is the only thing that can sustain it, for it is the only thing that can give us the resilience that we need if we are to evangelize boldly and persistently, and not be daunted by temporary setbacks. So far from being weakened by this faith, therefore, evangelism will inevitably be weak and lack staying power without it. This, I hope, will become clear as we proceed.

1

Divine Sovereignty

I do not intend to spend any time at all proving to you the general truth that God is sovereign in his world. There is no need; for I know that, if you are a Christian, you believe this already. How do I know that? Because I know that, if you are a Christian, you pray; and the recognition of God's sovereignty is the basis of your prayers. In prayer, you ask for things and give thanks for things. Why? Because you recognize that God is the author and source of all the good that you have had already, and all the good that you hope for in the future. This is the fundamental philosophy of Christian prayer. The prayer of a Christian is not an attempt to force God's hand, but a humble acknowledgment of helplessness and dependence. When we are on our knees, we know that it is not we who control the world; it is not in our power, therefore, to supply our needs by our own independent efforts; every good thing that we desire for ourselves and for others must be sought from God, and will come, if it comes at all, as a gift from his hands. If this is true even of our daily bread (and the Lord's Prayer teaches us that it is), much more is it true of spiritual benefits. This is all luminously clear to us when we are actually praying, whatever we may be betrayed into saying in argument afterward. In effect, therefore, what we do every time we pray is to confess our own impotence and God's sovereignty. The very fact that a Christian prays is thus proof positive that he believes in the lordship of his God.

Nor, again, am I going to spend time proving to you the particular truth that God is sovereign in salvation. For that, too, you believe already. Two facts show this. In the first place, you give God thanks for your conversion. Now why do you do that? Because you know in your heart that God was entirely responsible for it. You did not save yourself; he saved you. Your thanksgiving is itself an acknowledgment that your conversion was not your own work, but his work. You do not put it down to chance or accident that you came under Christian influence when you did. You do not put it down to chance or accident that you attended a Christian church, that you heard the Christian gospel, that you had Christian friends and, perhaps, a Christian home, that the Bible fell into your hands, that you saw your need of Christ and came to trust him as your Savior. You do not attribute your repenting and believing to your own wisdom, or prudence, or sound judgment, or good sense. Perhaps, in the days when you were seeking Christ, you labored and strove hard, read and pondered much, but all that outlay of effort did not make your conversion your own work. Your act of faith when you closed with Christ was yours in the sense that it was you.

who performed it; but that does not mean that you saved yourself. In fact, it never occurs to you to suppose that you saved yourself.

As you look back, you take to yourself the blame for your past blindness and indifference and obstinacy and evasiveness in face of the gospel message; but you do not pat yourself on the back for having been at length mastered by the insistent Christ. You would never dream of dividing the credit for your salvation between God and yourself. You have never for one moment supposed that the decisive contribution to your salvation was yours and not God's. You have never told God that, while you are grateful for the means and opportunities of grace that he gave you, you realize that you have to thank, not him, but yourself for the fact that you responded to his call. Your heart revolts at the very thought of talking to God in such terms. In fact, you thank him no less sincerely for the gift of faith and repentance than for the gift of a Christ to trust and turn to. This is the way in which, since you became a Christian, your heart has always led you. You give God all the glory for all that your salvation involved, and you know that it would be blasphemy if you refused to thank him for bringing you to faith. Thus, in the way that you think of your conversion and give thanks for your conversion, you acknowledge the sovereignty of divine grace. And every other Christian in the world does the same.

It is instructive in this connection to ponder Charles Simeon's account of his conversation with John Wesley on December 10, 1784 (the date is given in Wesley's journal): "Sir, I understand that you are called an Arminian; and I have been sometimes called a Calvinist; and therefore I suppose we are to draw daggers. But before I consent to begin the combat, with your permission I will ask you a few questions. . . . Pray, Sir, do you feel yourself a depraved creature, so depraved that you would never have thought of turning to God, if God had not first put it into your heart?" "Yes," says the veteran, "I do indeed." "And do you utterly despair of recommending yourself to God by anything you can do; and look for salvation solely through the blood and righteousness of Christ?" "Yes, solely through Christ." "But, Sir, supposing you were at first saved by Christ, are you not somehow or other to save yourself afterwards by your own works?" "No, I must be saved by Christ from first to last." "Allowing, then, that you were first turned by the grace of God, are you not in some way or other to keep yourself by your own power?" "No." "What, then, are you to be upheld every hour and every moment by God, as much as an infant in its mother's arms?" "Yes, altogether." "And is all your hope in the grace and mercy of God to preserve you unto his heavenly kingdom?" "Yes, I have no hope but in him." "Then, Sir, with your leave I will put up my dagger again; for this is all my Calvinism; this is my election, my justification by faith, my final perseverance: it is in substance all that I hold, and as I hold it; and therefore, if you please, instead of searching out terms and phrases to be a ground of contention between us, we will cordially unite in those things wherein we agree."[1]

There is a second way in which you acknowledge that God

---

[1] *Horae Homileticae*, Preface: i.xvii-xviii.

is sovereign in salvation. You pray for the conversion of others. In what terms, now, do you intercede for them? Do you limit yourself to asking that God will bring them to a point where they can save themselves, independently of him? I do not think you do. I think that what you do is to pray in categorical terms that God will, quite simply and decisively, save them: that he will open the eyes of their understanding, soften their hard hearts, renew their natures, and move their wills to receive the Savior. You ask God to work in them everything necessary for their salvation. You would not dream of making it a point in your prayer that you are not asking God actually to bring them to faith, because you recognize that that is something he cannot do. Nothing of the sort! When you pray for unconverted people, you do so on the assumption that it is in God's power to bring them to faith. You entreat him to do that very thing, and your confidence in asking rests on the certainty that he is able to do what you ask. And so indeed he is: this conviction, which animates your intercessions, is God's own truth, written on your heart by the Holy Spirit. In prayer, then (and the Christian is at his sanest and wisest when he prays), you know that it is God who saves men; you know that what makes men turn to God is God's own gracious work of drawing them to himself; and the content of your prayers is determined by this knowledge. Thus, by your practice of intercession, no less than by giving thanks for your conversion, you acknowledge and confess the sovereignty of God's grace. And so do all Christian people everywhere.

There is a long-standing controversy in the church as to whether God is really Lord in relation to human conduct and saving faith or not. What has been said shows us how we should regard this controversy. The situation is not what it seems to be. For it is not true that some Christians believe in divine sovereignty while others hold an opposite view. What is true is that all Christians believe in divine sovereignty, but some are not aware that they do, and mistakenly imagine and insist that they reject it. What causes this odd state of affairs? The root cause is the same as in most cases of error in the church—the intruding of rationalistic speculations, the passion for systematic consistency, a reluctance to recognize the existence of mystery and to let God be wiser than men, and a consequent subjecting of Scripture to the supposed demands of human logic. People see that the Bible teaches man's responsibility for his actions; they do not see (man, indeed, cannot see) how this is consistent with the sovereign lordship of God over those actions. They are not content to let the two truths live side by side, as they do in the Scriptures, but jump to the conclusion that, in order to uphold the biblical truth of human responsibility, they are bound to reject the equally biblical and equally true doctrine of divine sovereignty, and to explain away the great number of texts that teach it. The desire to oversimplify the Bible by cutting out the mysteries is natural to our perverse minds, and it is not surprising that even good people should fall victim to it. Hence this persistent and troublesome dispute. The irony of the situation, however, is that when we ask how the two sides pray, it becomes apparent that those who profess to deny God's sovereignty really believe in it just as strongly as those who affirm it.

How, then, do you pray? Do you ask God for your daily bread? Do you thank God for your conversion? Do you pray for the conversion of others? If the answer is "no," I can only say that I do not think you are yet born again. But if the answer is "yes"—well, that proves that, whatever side you may have taken in debates on this question in the past, in your heart you believe in the sovereignty of God no less firmly than anyone else. On our feet we may have arguments about it, but on our knees we are all agreed. And it is this common agreement, of which our prayers give proof, that I take as our starting point now.

2

DIVINE SOVEREIGNTY AND HUMAN RESPONSIBILITY

Our aim in the present study is to think out the nature of the Christian's evangelistic task in the light of this agreed presupposition that God is sovereign in salvation. Now, we need to recognize right at the outset that this is no easy assignment. All theological topics contain pitfalls for the unwary, for God's truth is never quite what man would have expected; and our present subject is more treacherous than most. This is because in thinking it through we have to deal with an antinomy in the biblical revelation, and in such circumstances our finite, fallen minds are more than ordinarily apt to go astray.

What is an antinomy? The *Shorter Oxford English Dictionary* defines it as "a contradiction between conclusions which seem equally logical, reasonable or necessary." For our purposes, however, this definition is not quite accurate; the opening words should read "an appearance of contradiction." For the whole point of an antinomy—in theology, at any rate—is that it is not a real contradiction, though it looks like one. It is an apparent incompatibility between two apparent truths. An antinomy exists when a pair of principles stand side by side, seemingly irreconcilable, yet both undeniable. There are cogent reasons for believing each of them; each rests on clear and solid evidence; but it is a mystery to you how they can be squared with each other. You see that each must be true on its own, but you do not see how they can both be true together. Let me give an example. Modern physics faces an antinomy, in this sense, in its study of light. There is cogent evidence to show that light consists of waves, and equally cogent evidence to show that it consists of particles. It is not apparent how light can be both waves and particles, but the evidence is there, and so neither view can be ruled out in favor of the other. Neither, however, can be reduced to the other or explained in terms of the other; the two seemingly incompatible positions must be held together, and both must be treated as true. Such a necessity scandalizes our tidy minds, no doubt, but there is no help for it if we are to be loyal to the facts.

It appears, therefore, that an antinomy is not the same thing as a paradox. A paradox is a figure of speech, a play on words. It is a form of statement that seems to unite two opposite ideas, or to deny something by the very terms in which it is asserted. Many truths about the Christian life can be expressed as paradoxes. A *Book of Common Prayer* collect, for instance, declares that God's "service is perfect freedom":

man goes free through becoming a slave. Paul states various paradoxes of his own Christian experience: "sorrowful, yet always rejoicing; as poor, yet making many rich; as having nothing, yet possessing everything"; "when I am weak, then I am strong" (2 Cor 6:10; 12:10). The point of a paradox, however, is that what creates the appearance of contradiction is not the facts, but the words. The contradiction is verbal, but not real, and a little thought shows how it can be eliminated and the same idea expressed in nonparadoxical form. In other words a paradox is always *dispensable*. Look at the examples quoted. The *Book of Common Prayer* might have said that those who serve God are free from sin's dominion. In 2 Corinthians 6:10 Paul might have said that sorrow at circumstances and joy in God are constantly combined in his experience, and that, though he owns no property and has no bank balance, there is a sense in which everything belongs to him, because he is Christ's, and Christ is Lord of all. Again, in 2 Corinthians 12:10, he might have said that the Lord strengthens him most when he is most conscious of his natural infirmity. Such nonparadoxical forms of speech are clumsy and dull beside the paradoxes which they would replace, but they express precisely the same meaning. For a paradox is merely a matter of how you use words; the employment of paradox is an arresting trick of speech, but it does not imply even an appearance of contradiction in the facts that you are describing.

Also it should be noted that a paradox is always *comprehensible*. A speaker or writer casts his ideas into paradoxes in order to make them memorable and provoke thought about them. But the person at the receiving end must be able, on reflection, to see how to unravel the paradox, otherwise it will seem to him to be really self-contradictory, and therefore really meaningless. An incomprehensible paradox could not be distinguished from a mere contradiction in terms. Sheer paradox would thus have to be written off as sheer nonsense.

By contrast, however, an antinomy is neither dispensable nor comprehensible. It is not a figure of speech, but an observed relation between two statements of fact. It is not deliberately manufactured; it is forced on us by the facts themselves. It is unavoidable, and it is insoluble. We do not invent it, and we cannot explain it. Nor is there any way to get rid of it, save by falsifying the very facts that led us to it.

What should one do, then, with an antinomy? Accept it for what it is, and learn to live with it. Refuse to regard the apparent inconsistency as real; put down the semblance of contradiction to the deficiency of your own understanding; think of the two principles as not rival alternatives but, in some way that at present you do not grasp, complementary to each other. Be careful, therefore, not to set them at loggerheads, nor to make deductions from either that would cut across the other (such deductions would, for that very reason, be certainly unsound). Use each within the limits of its own sphere of reference (i.e., the area delimited by the evidence from which the principle has been drawn). Note what connections exist between the two truths and their two frames of reference, and teach yourself to think of reality in a way that provides for their peaceful coexistence, remembering that reality itself has proved actually to contain them both. This is how antinomies must be handled, whether in nature or in Scripture. This, as I understand it, is how modern physics deals with the problem of light, and this is how Christians have to deal with the antinomies of biblical teaching.

The particular antinomy which concerns us here is the apparent opposition between divine sovereignty and human responsibility, or (putting it more biblically) between what God does as King and what he does as Judge. Scripture teaches that, as King, he orders and controls all things, human actions among them, in accordance with his own eternal purpose (see Gen 14:8; 50:20; Prov 16:9; 21:1; Mt 10:29; Acts 9:27-28; Rom 9:20-21; Eph 1:11, etc.). Scripture also teaches that, as Judge, he holds every man responsible for the choices he makes and the courses of action he pursues (see Mt 25; Rom 2:1-16; Rev 20:11-13, etc.). Thus, hearers of the gospel are responsible for their reaction; if they reject the good news, they are guilty of unbelief. "Whoever does not believe is condemned already, because he has not believed" (Jn 3:18; cf. Mt 11:20-24; Acts 13:38-41; 2 Thess 1:7-10, etc.). Again, Paul, entrusted with the gospel, is responsible for preaching it; if he neglects his commission, he is penalized for unfaithfulness. "Necessity is laid upon me. Woe to me if I do not preach the gospel!" (1 Cor 9:16; cf. Ezek 3:17ff.; 33:7ff.). God's sovereignty and man's responsibility are taught to us side by side in the same Bible; sometimes, indeed, in the same text.[1] Both are thus guaranteed to

---

[1] E.g., Lk 22:22: "For the Son of Man goes as it has been determined (to his death), but woe to that man by whom he is betrayed!" Cf. Acts 2:23.

us by the same divine authority; both, therefore, are true. It follows that they must be held together, and not played off against each other. Man is a responsible moral agent, though he is also divinely controlled; man is divinely controlled, though he is also a responsible moral agent. God's sovereignty is a reality, and man's responsibility is a reality too. This is the revealed antinomy in terms of which we have to do our thinking about evangelism.

To our finite minds, of course, the thing is inexplicable. It sounds like a contradiction, and our first reaction is to complain that it is absurd. Paul notices this complaint in Romans 9. "You will say to me then, 'Why does he [God] still find fault? For who can resist his will?'" (Rom 9:19). If, as our Lord, God orders all our actions, how can it be reasonable or right for him to act also as our Judge, and condemn our shortcomings? Observe how Paul replies. He does not attempt to demonstrate the propriety of God's action; instead, he rebukes the spirit of the question. "But who are you, O man, to answer back to God?" What the objector has to learn is that he, a creature and a sinner, has no right whatsoever to find fault with the revealed ways of God. Creatures are not entitled to register complaints about their Creator. As Paul goes on to say, God's sovereignty is wholly just, for his right to dispose of his creatures is absolute (Rom 9:20-21). Earlier in the epistle, he had shown that God's judgment of sinners is also wholly just, since our sins richly deserve his sentence (Rom 1:18ff., 32; 2:1-16). Our part, he would tell us, is to acknowledge these facts, and to adore God's righteousness, both as King and as Judge; not to speculate as to how his just sovereignty can be consistent with his just judgment, and certainly not to call the justice of either in question because we find the problem of their relationship too hard for us! Our speculations are not the measure of our God. The Creator has told us that he is both a sovereign Lord and a righteous Judge, and that should be enough for us. Why do we hesitate to take his word for it? Can we not trust what he says?

We ought not, in any case, to be surprised when we find mysteries of this sort in God's Word. For the Creator is incomprehensible to his creatures. A God whom we could understand exhaustively, and whose revelation of himself confronted us with no mysteries whatsoever, would be a God in man's image and therefore an imaginary God, not the God of the Bible at all. For what the God of the Bible says is this: "my thoughts are not your thoughts, / neither are your ways my ways, declares the Lord. / For as the heavens are higher than the earth, / so are my ways higher than your ways / and my thoughts than your thoughts" (Is 55:8-9). The antinomy which we face now is only one of a number that the Bible contains. We may be sure that they all find their reconciliation in the mind and counsel of God, and we may hope that in heaven we shall understand them ourselves. But meanwhile, our wisdom is to maintain with equal emphasis both the apparently conflicting truths in each case, to hold them together in the relation in which the Bible itself sets them, and to recognize that here is a mystery which we cannot expect to solve in this world.

This is easily said, but the thing is not easily done. For our minds dislike antinomies. We like to tie up everything into neat intellectual parcels, with all appearance of mystery dispelled and no loose ends hanging out. Hence we are tempted to get rid of antinomies from our minds by illegitimate means: to suppress, or jettison, one truth in the supposed interests of the other, and for the sake of a tidier theology. So it is in the present case. The temptation is to undercut and maim the one truth by the way in which we stress the other: to assert man's responsibility in a way that excludes God from being sovereign, or to affirm God's sovereignty in a way that destroys the responsibility of man. Both mistakes need to be guarded against. It is worth reflecting, therefore, on the way in which these temptations arise in connection specifically with evangelism.

There is, first, the temptation to *an exclusive concern with human responsibility*. As we have seen, human responsibility is a fact, and a very solemn fact. Man's responsibility to his Maker is, indeed, the fundamental fact of his life, and it can never be taken too seriously. God made us responsible moral agents, and he will not treat us as anything less. His Word addresses each of us individually, and each of us is responsible for the way in which he responds—for his attention or inattention, his belief or unbelief, his obedience or disobedience. We cannot evade responsibility for our reaction to God's revelation. We live under his law. We must answer to him for our lives.

Man without Christ is a guilty sinner, answerable to God for breaking his law. That is why he needs the gospel. When he hears the gospel, he is responsible for the decision that he makes about it. It sets before him a choice between life and death, the most momentous choice that any man can ever face. When we present the gospel to an unconverted man, it is very likely that, without fully realizing what he is doing, he will try to blind himself to the gravity of this issue, and thereby to justify himself in shrugging the whole thing off. Then we have to use every legitimate means in our power to bring home to him the seriousness of the choice that confronts him, and to urge him not to let himself treat so solemn a matter in an irresponsible way. When we preach the promises and invitations of the gospel, and offer Christ to sinful men and women, it is part of our task to emphasize and re-emphasize that they are responsible to God for the way in which they react to the good news of his grace. No preacher can ever make this point too strongly.

Similarly, we ourselves have a responsibility for making the gospel known. Christ's command to his disciples, "Go . . . and make disciples of all nations" (Mt 28:19), was spoken to them in their representative capacity; this is Christ's command, not merely to the apostles, but to the whole Church. Evangelism is the inalienable responsibility of every Christian community, and every Christian person. We are all under orders to devote ourselves to spreading the good news, and to use all our ingenuity and enterprise to bring it to the notice of the whole world. The Christian, therefore, must constantly be searching his conscience, asking himself if he is doing all that he might be doing in this field. For this also is a responsibility that cannot be shrugged off.

It is necessary, therefore, to take the thought of human responsibility, as it affects both the preacher and the hearer of the gospel, very seriously indeed. But we must not let it drive the thought of divine sovereignty out of our minds. While we must always remember that it is our responsibility to proclaim salvation, we must never forget that it is God who saves. It is God who brings men and women under the sound of the gospel, and it is God who brings them to faith in Christ. Our evangelistic work is the instrument that he uses for this purpose, but the power that saves is not in the instrument: it is in the hand of the One who uses the instrument. We must not at any stage forget that. For if we forget that it is God's prerogative to give results when the gospel is preached, we shall start to think that it is our responsibility to secure them. And if we forget that only God can give faith, we shall start to think that the making of converts depends, in the last analysis, not on God, but on us, and that the decisive factor is the way in which we evangelize. And this line of thought, consistently followed through, will lead us far astray.

Let us work this out. If we regarded it as our job, not simply to present Christ, but actually to produce converts—to evangelize, not only faithfully, but also successfully—our approach to evangelism would become pragmatic and calculating. We should conclude that our basic equipment, both for personal dealing and for public preaching, must be twofold. We must have not merely a clear grasp of the meaning and application of the gospel but also an irresistible technique for inducing a response. We should, therefore, make it our business to try and develop such a technique. And we should evaluate all evangelism, our own and other people's, by the criterion not only of the message preached but also of visible results. If our own efforts were not bearing fruit, we should conclude that our technique still needed improving. If they were bearing fruit, we should conclude that this justified the technique we had been using. We should regard evangelism as an activity involving a battle of wills between ourselves and those to whom we go, a battle in which victory depends on our firing off a heavy enough barrage of calculated effects. Thus our philosophy of evangelism would become terrifyingly similar to the philosophy of brainwashing. And we would no longer be able to argue, when such a similarity is asserted to be a fact, that this is not a proper conception of evangelism.[2] For it would be a proper conception of evangelism if the production of converts was really our responsibility.

This shows us the danger of forgetting the practical implications of God's sovereignty. It is right to recognize our responsibility to engage in aggressive evangelism. It is right to desire the conversion of unbelievers. It is right to want one's presentation of the gospel to be as clear and forcible as possible. If we preferred that converts should be few and far between, and did not care whether our proclaiming of Christ went home or not, there would be something wrong with us. But it is not right when we take it on us to do more than God has given us to do. It is not right when we regard ourselves as responsible for securing converts, and look to our own enterprise and techniques to accomplish what only God can

---

[2]As D. M. Lloyd-Jones argues in *Conversions: Psychological and Spiritual* (I.V.F., 1959), against the thesis of Dr. William Sargant.

accomplish. To do that is to intrude ourselves into the office of the Holy Spirit, and to exalt ourselves as the agents of the new birth. And the point that we must see is this: *only by letting our knowledge of God's sovereignty control the way in which we plan, and pray, and work in his service, can we avoid becoming guilty of this fault.* For where we are not consciously relying on God, there we shall inevitably be found relying on ourselves. And the spirit of self-reliance is a blight on evangelism. Such, however, is the inevitable consequence of forgetting God's sovereignty in the conversion of souls.

But there is an opposite temptation that threatens us also: namely, the temptation to *an exclusive concern with divine sovereignty.*

There are some Christians whose minds are constantly taken up with thoughts of the sovereignty of God, This truth means a great deal to them. It has come to them quite suddenly, perhaps, and with the force of a tremendous revelation. They would say that it has caused a real Copernican revolution in their outlook; it has given a new center to their entire personal universe. Previously, as they now see, man had been central in their universe, and God had been on the circumference. They had thought of him as a spectator of events in his world, rather than as their author. They had assumed that the controlling factor in every situation was man's handling of it rather than God's plan for it, and they had looked on the happiness of human beings as the most interesting and important thing in creation, for God no less than for themselves. But now they see that this man-centered outlook was sinful and unbiblical; they see that, from one standpoint, the whole purpose of the Bible is to overthrow it, and that books like Deuteronomy and Isaiah and John's Gospel and Romans smash it to smithereens in almost every chapter; and they realize that henceforth God must be central in their thoughts and concerns, just as he is central in reality in his own world. Now they feel the force of the famous first answer in the Westminster *Shorter Catechism*: "Man's chief end is to glorify God, and [by so doing, and in so doing,] to enjoy him for ever." Now they see that the way to find the happiness that God promises is not to seek it as an end in itself, but to forget oneself in the daily preoccupation of seeking God's glory and doing his will and proving his power through the ups and downs and stresses and strains of everyday life. They see that it is the glory and praise of God that must absorb them henceforth, for time and for eternity. They see that the whole purpose of their existence is that with heart and life they should worship and exalt God. In every situation, therefore, their one question is: what will make the most for God's glory? What should I do in order that in these circumstances God may be magnified?

And they see, as they ask this question, that, though God uses men as means for achieving his purposes, in the last analysis nothing depends on man; everything depends, rather, on the God who raises men up to do his will. They see, too, that God is handling every situation before his servants come on the scene, and that he continues to handle it and work out his will in it through each thing that they do— through their mistakes and failures, no less than through their personal successes. They see, therefore, that they need never fear for the ark of God, as Uzzah feared for it, for God will maintain his own cause. They see that they need never make Uzzah's mistake, of taking too much on them, and doing God's work in a forbidden way for fear that otherwise it would not get done at all (2 Sam 6:6-7).[3] They see that, since God is always in control, they need never fear that they will expose him to loss and damage if they limit themselves to serving him in the way that he has appointed. They see that any other supposition would in effect be a denial of his wisdom, or his sovereignty, or both. They see, also, that the Christian must never for one moment imagine himself to be indispensable to God, or allow himself to behave as if he were. The God who sent him, and is pleased to work with him, can do without him. He must be ready to spend and be spent in the tasks that God sets him; but he must never suppose that the loss to the church would be irreparable if God should lay him aside and use someone else. He must not at any point say to himself, "God's cause would collapse without me and the work I am doing"—for there is never any reason to think this is so. It is never true that God would be at a loss without you and me. Those who have begun to understand the sovereignty of God see all this, and so they seek to efface themselves in all their work for God. They thus bear a practical witness to their belief that God is great, and reigns, by trying to make themselves small, and to act in a way which is itself an acknowledgment that the fruitfulness of their Christian service depends wholly on God, and not on themselves. And up to this point they are right.

They are, however, beset by exactly the opposite tempta-

---

[3]Uzzah transgressed the prohibition of Num 4:5.

tion to that discussed above. In their zeal to glorify God by acknowledging his sovereignty in grace, and by refusing to imagine that their own services are indispensable to him, they are tempted to lose sight of the church's responsibility to evangelize. Their temptation is to reason thus: "Agreed, the world is ungodly; but, surely, the less we do about it, the more God will be glorified when at length he breaks in to restore the situation. The most important thing for us to do is to take care that we leave the initiative in his hands." They are tempted, therefore, to suspect all enterprise in evangelism, whether organized or on the personal level, as if there were something essentially and inescapably man-exalting about it. They are haunted by the fear of running ahead of God, and feel that there is nothing more urgent than to guard against the possibility of doing this.

Perhaps the classic instance of this way of thinking was provided two centuries ago by the chairman of the ministers' fraternal at which William Carey mooted the founding of a missionary society. "Sit down, young man," said the old warrior; "when God is pleased to convert the heathen, He will do it without your aid, or mine!" The idea of taking the initiative in going out to find men of all nations for Christ struck him as improper and, indeed, presumptuous.

Now, think twice before you condemn that old man. He was not entirely without understanding. He had at least grasped that it is God who saves, and that he saves according to his own purpose, and does not take orders from man in the matter. He had grasped too that we must never suppose that without our help God would be helpless. He had, in other words, learned to take the sovereignty of God perfectly seriously. His mistake was that he was not taking the church's evangelistic responsibility with equal seriousness. He was forgetting that God's way of saving men is to send out his servants to tell them the gospel, and that the church has been charged to go into all the world for that very purpose.

But this is something that we must not forget. Christ's command means that we all should be devoting all our resources of ingenuity and enterprise to the task of making the gospel known in every possible way to every possible person. Unconcern and inaction with regard to evangelism are always, therefore, inexcusable. And the doctrine of divine sovereignty would be grossly misapplied if we should invoke it in such a way as to lessen the urgency, and immediacy, and priority, and binding constraint, of the evangelistic imperative. No revealed truth may be invoked to extenuate sin. God did not teach us the reality of his rule in order to give us an excuse for neglecting his orders.

In our Lord's parable of the talents (Mt 25:14-30), the "good and faithful" servants were those who furthered their master's interests by making the most enterprising lawful use that they could of what was entrusted to them. The servant who buried his talent, and did nothing with it beyond keeping it intact, no doubt imagined that he was being extremely good and faithful, but his master judged him to be "wicked," "slothful" and "unprofitable." For what Christ has given us to use must be put to use; it is not enough simply to hide it away. We may apply this to our stewardship of the gospel. The truth about salvation has been made known to us, not for us simply to preserve (though we must certainly do that), but also, and primarily, for us to spread. The light is not meant to be hidden under the bushel. It is meant to shine; and it is our business to see that it shines. "You are the light of the world," says our Lord (Mt 5:14-16). He who does not devote himself to evangelism in every way that he can is not, therefore, playing the part of a good and faithful servant of Jesus Christ.

Here, then, are two opposite pitfalls: a Scylla and Charybdis of error. Each is the result of partial vision, which means partial blindness; each reveals a failure to face squarely the biblical antinomy of the responsibility of man and the sovereignty of God. Both unite to warn us not to pit these truths against each other, nor to allow either to obscure or overshadow the other in our minds. Both unite to warn us also against reacting from one extreme of error into the other. If we did that, our last state might well be worse than the first. What are we to do, then? To direct our course along the narrow channel that leads between Scylla and Charybdis; in other words, to avoid both extremes. How? By making it our business to believe both these doctrines with all our might, and to keep both constantly before us for the guidance and government of our lives.

We shall proceed now according to this maxim. In what follows, we shall try to take both doctrines perfectly seriously, as the Bible does, and to view them in their positive biblical relationship. We shall not oppose them to each other, for the Bible does not oppose them to each other. Nor shall we qualify, or modify, or water down, either of them in terms of the other, for this is not what the Bible does either. What the Bible does is to assert both truths side by side in the strongest and most unambiguous terms as two ultimate facts; this, therefore, is the position that we must take in our own thinking. C. H. Spurgeon was once asked if he could reconcile these two truths to each other. "I wouldn't try," he replied; "I never reconcile friends." Friends?—yes, friends. This is the point that we have to grasp. In the Bible, divine sovereignty and human responsibility are not enemies. They are not uneasy neighbors; they are not in an endless state of cold war with each other. They are friends, and they work together. I hope that what I am to say now about evangelism will help to make this clear.

3

EVANGELISM

We shall now try to answer from Scripture the following four questions concerning the Christian's evangelistic responsibility. What is evangelism? What is the evangelistic message? What is the motive for evangelizing? By what means and methods should evangelism be practiced?

WHAT IS EVANGELISM?

It might be expected that evangelical Christians would not need to spend time discussing this question. In view of the emphasis that evangelicals always, and rightly, lay on the primacy of evangelism, it would be natural to assume that we were all perfectly unanimous as to what evangelism is. Yet, in fact, much of the confusion in present-day debates about evangelism arises from lack of agreement at this point. The root of the confusion can be stated in a sentence. It is our widespread and persistent habit of defining evangelism in terms, not of a message delivered, but of an effect produced in our hearers.

For illustration of this, look at the famous definition of evangelism which the Archbishops' Committee gave in its report on the evangelistic work of the Church in 1918. "To *evangelize*," declared the Committee, "is *so to present Christ Jesus in the power of the Holy Spirit, that men shall come to put their trust in God through him, to accept him as their Savior, and serve him as their King in the fellowship of his Church*."

Now this is in many ways an excellent definition. It states admirably the aim and purpose of the evangelistic enterprise, and rules out many inadequate and misleading ideas. To start with, it makes the point that evangelizing means *declaring a specific message.* According to this definition, it is not evangelism merely to teach general truths about God's existence or the moral law; evangelism means *to present Christ Jesus,* the divine Son who became man at a particular point in world history in order to save a ruined race. Nor, according to this definition, is it evangelism merely to present the teaching and example of the historical Jesus, or even the truth about his saving work; evangelism means to present Christ Jesus himself, the living Savior and the reigning Lord. Nor, again, is it evangelism, according to this definition, merely to set forth the living Jesus as Helper and Friend, without reference to his saving work on the cross; evangelism means to present Jesus as Christ, God's anointed Servant, fulfilling the tasks of his appointed office as Priest and King. "The man Christ Jesus" is to be presented as the "one mediator between God and men" (1 Tim 2:5), who "suffered once for sins . . . that he might bring us to God" (1 Pet 3:18) the One through whom, and through whom alone, men may come to put their trust in God, according to his own claim: "I am the way, and the truth, and the life. No one comes to the Father except through me" (Jn 14:6). He is to be proclaimed as the *Savior,* the One who "came into the world to save sinners" (1 Tim 1:15) and "redeemed us from the curse of the law by becoming a curse for us" (Gal 3:13)—"Jesus who delivers us from the wrath to come" (1 Thess 1:10 RSV). And he is to be set forth as King: "For to this end Christ died and lived again, that he might be Lord both of the dead and of the living" (Rom 14:9 RSV). There is no evangelism where this specific message is not declared.

Again, the definition makes the point that evangelizing means declaring this specific message *with a specific application.* It is not evangelism, according to this definition, to present Christ Jesus as a subject for detached critical and comparative study. Evangelism, according to this definition, means presenting Christ Jesus and his work in relation to the needs of fallen men and women, who are without God as a Father and under the wrath of God as a Judge. Evangelism means presenting Christ Jesus to them as their only hope, in this world or the next. Evangelism means exhorting sinners to *accept* Christ Jesus *as their Savior,* recognizing that in the most final and far-reaching sense they are lost without him. Nor is this all. Evangelism also means summoning men to receive Christ Jesus as all that he is—Lord, as well as Savior—and therefore to *serve him as their King in the fellowship of his church,* the company of those who worship him, witness to him, and work for him here on earth. In other words, evangelism is the issuing of a call to turn, as well as to trust; it is the delivering, not merely of a divine invitation to receive a Savior, but of a divine command to repent of sin. And there is no evangelism where this specific application is not made.

The definition under review establishes these vital points well. But on one fundamental matter it goes astray. It puts a consecutive clause where a final clause should be. Had it begun: "to evangelize is to present Christ Jesus to sinful men in order that, through the power of the Holy Spirit, they may come," there would be no fault to find with it. But it does not say this. What it does say is quite different. "To evangelize is so to present Christ Jesus in the power of the Holy Spirit, that men shall come." This is to define evangelism in terms of an effect achieved in the lives of others; which amounts to saying that the essence of evangelizing is producing converts.

But this cannot be right, as we pointed out at an earlier stage. Evangelism is man's work, but the giving of faith is God's. It is true, indeed, that every evangelist's aim is to convert, and that our definition perfectly expresses the ideal which he longs to see fulfilled in his own ministry; but the question whether or not one is evangelizing cannot be settled simply by asking whether one has had conversions. There have been missionaries to Muslims who labored for a lifetime and saw no converts; must we conclude from this that they were not evangelizing? There have been un-evangelical preachers through whose words (not always understood in the sense intended) individuals have been soundly converted; must we conclude from this that these preachers were evangelizing after all? The answer, surely, is no in both cases. The results of preaching depend, not on the wishes and intentions of men, but on the will of God Almighty.

This consideration does not mean that we should be indifferent as to whether we see fruit from our witness to Christ or not; if fruit is not appearing, we should seek God's face about it to find out why. But this consideration does mean that we ought not to define evangelism in terms of achieved results.

How, then, should evangelism be defined? The New Testament answer is very simple. According to the New Testament, evangelism is just preaching the gospel, the evangel. It is a work of communication in which Christians make themselves mouthpieces for God's message of mercy to sinners. Anyone who faithfully delivers that message, under whatever circumstances, in a large meeting, in a small meeting, from a pulpit, or in a private conversation, is evangelizing. Since the divine message finds its climax in a plea from the Creator to a rebel world to turn and put faith in Christ, the delivering of it involves the summoning of one's hearers to conversion. If you are not, in this sense, seeking to bring about conversions, you are not evangelizing; this we have seen already. But the way to tell whether in fact you are evangelizing is not to ask whether conversions are known to have resulted from your witness. It is to ask whether you are faithfully making known the gospel message.

For a complete picture of what the New Testament means by evangelism, we need not look further than the apostle Paul's account of the nature of his own evangelistic ministry. There are three points to note about it.

1. Paul evangelized as the commissioned representative of the Lord Jesus Christ. Evangelism was a task that had been specifically entrusted to him. "Christ . . . [sent] me . . . to preach the gospel" (1 Cor 1:17). Now, see how he regarded himself in virtue of this commission. In the first place, he saw himself as Christ's steward. "This is how one should regard us [myself, and my fellow-preacher Apollos]," he wrote to the Corinthians, "as servants of Christ, and [in that capacity] stewards of the mysteries of God" (1 Cor 4:1 RSV). "I am . . . entrusted with a stewardship [of the gospel]" (1 Cor 9:17). Paul saw himself as a bondslave raised to a position of high trust, as the steward of a household in New Testament times always was; he had been "approved by God to be entrusted with the gospel" (1 Thess 2:4 RSV; cf. 1 Tim 1:11-12; Tit 1:3), and the responsibility now rested on him to be faithful to his trust, as a steward must be (cf. 1 Cor 4:2), guarding the precious truth that had been committed to him (as he later charges Timothy to do [1 Tim 6:20; 2 Tim 1:13-14]), and distributing and dispensing it according to his Master's instructions. The fact that he had been entrusted with this stewardship meant, as he told the Corinthians, that "necessity is laid upon me. Woe to me if I do not preach the gospel!" (1 Cor 9:16; cf. Acts 20:20, 26-27; 2 Cor 5:10-11; Ezek 3:16ff.; 33:7ff.). The figure of stewardship thus highlights Paul's *responsibility* to evangelize.

Again, Paul saw himself as Christ's *herald*. When he describes himself as "appointed a preacher" of the gospel (2 Tim 1:11; 1 Tim 2:7 RSV), the noun he uses is *kēryx*, which means a herald, a person who makes public announcements on another's behalf. When he declares, "we preach Christ crucified" (1 Cor 1:23), the verb he uses is *kēryssō*, which denotes the herald's appointed activity of blazoning abroad what he has been told to make known. When Paul speaks of "my *preaching*," and "our *preaching*," and lays it down that, after the world's wisdom had rendered the world ignorant of God, "it pleased God by the foolishness of preaching to save them that believe" (1 Cor 1:21; 2:4; 15:14 KJV), the noun he uses is *kērygma*, meaning not the activity of announcing, but the thing announced, the proclamation itself, the message declared. Paul, in his own estimation, was not a philosopher, not a moralist, not one of the world's wise men, but simply Christ's herald. His royal Master had given him a message to proclaim; his whole business, therefore, was to deliver that message with exact and studious faithfulness, adding nothing, altering nothing, and omitting nothing. And he was to deliver it, not as another of man's bright ideas, needing to be beautified with the cosmetics and high heels of fashionable learning in order to make people look at it, but as a word from God, spoken in Christ's name, carrying Christ's authority, and to be authenticated in the hearers by the convincing power of Christ's Spirit. "And I, when I came to you," Paul reminds the Corinthians, "[came] proclaiming to you the testimony of God." I came, Paul is saying, not to give you my own ideas about anything, but simply to deliver God's message. Therefore, "I decided to know nothing among you except Jesus Christ and him crucified"—for it was just this that God sent me to tell you about. "And my speech and my message [*kērygma*] were not in plausible words of wisdom, but in demonstration of the Spirit and of power, that your faith might not rest in the wisdom of men but in the power of God" (1 Cor 2:1-5 KJV). The figure of the herald thus highlights the *authenticity* of Paul's gospel.

Third, Paul considered himself Christ's *ambassador*. What is an ambassador? He is the authorized representative of a sovereign. He speaks not in his own name, but on behalf of the ruler whose deputy he is, and his whole duty and responsibility is to interpret that ruler's mind faithfully to those to whom he is sent. Paul used this figure twice, both times in connection with his evangelistic work. Pray for me, he wrote from prison, "that utterance may be given me in opening my mouth boldly to proclaim the mystery of the gospel, for which I am an *ambassador* in chains; that I may declare it boldly, as I ought to speak." God, he wrote again, has "entrust[ed] to us the message of reconciliation. So we are *ambassadors* for Christ, God making his appeal through us. We beseech you on behalf of Christ, be reconciled to God" (Eph 6:19-20 RSV; 2 Cor 5:19-20 RSV). Paul called himself an ambassador because he knew that, when he proclaimed the gospel facts and promises, and urged sinners to receive the reconciliation effected at Calvary, it was Christ's message to the world that he was declaring. The figure of ambassadorship thus highlights the *authority* that Paul had, as representing his Lord.

In his evangelism, then, Paul consciously acted as the slave and steward, the mouthpiece and herald, the spokesman and ambassador, of the Lord Jesus Christ. Hence, on the one hand, his sustained boldness and unshakable sense of authority in the face of ridicule and indifference; hence, on the other hand, his intransigent refusal to modify his message in order to suit circumstances. These two things, of course, were connected, for Paul could regard himself as speaking with Christ's authority only as long as he remained faithful to the terms of his commission and said neither less nor more than he had been given to say (cf. Gal 1:8ff). But while he preached the gospel that Christ had entrusted to him, he spoke as Christ's commissioned representative, and could therefore speak authoritatively, and claim a right to be heard.

But the commission to publish the gospel and make disciples was never confined to the apostles. Nor is it now confined to the church's ministers. It is a commission that rests on the whole church collectively, and therefore on each Christian individually. All God's people are sent to do as the Philippians did, and "shine as lights in the world, holding fast to the word of life" (Phil 2:15-16). Every Christian, therefore, has a God-given obligation to make known the gospel of Christ. And every Christian who declares the gospel message to any other person does so as Christ's ambassador and representative, according to the terms of his God-given commission. Such is the authority, and such the responsibility, of the church and of the Christian in evangelism.

The second point in Paul's understanding of his own evangelistic ministry follows on from the first.

2. *His primary task in evangelism was to teach the truth about the Lord Jesus Christ.* As Christ's ambassador, Paul's first job was to "get across" the message that his Sovereign had charged him to deliver. Christ sent me, he declared—to do what?—"to preach the gospel" (1 Cor 1:17). The Greek word here is *euangelizomai*, meaning publish the *euangelion*, literally the "good news." For that is what Paul's gospel was. Good news, Paul proclaimed, has come into the world—good news from God. It is unlike anything that the world,

Jewish or Gentile, had guessed or expected, but it is something that the whole world needs. This good news, the "word of God" in the usual New Testament sense of that phrase (cf. Acts 4:31; 8:14; 11:1; 13:46; 2 Cor 2:17; Col 1:25; 1 Thess 2:13; 2 Tim 2:9), "the truth" as Paul often called it (cf. 2 Cor 4:2; Gal 2:5, 14; 2 Thess 2:10ff.; 2 Tim 2:18, 25; 3:8), is a full and final disclosure of what the Creator has done, and will do, to save sinners. It is a complete unfolding of the spiritual facts of life in God's apostate world.

What was this good news that Paul preached? It was the news about Jesus of Nazareth. It was the news of the incarnation, the atonement and the kingdom—the cradle, the cross and the crown—of the Son of God. It was the news of how God "glorified his servant Jesus" (Acts 3:13 RSV) by making him Christ, the world's long-awaited "Leader and Savior" (Acts 5:31). It was the news of how God made his Son man; and how, as man, God made him Priest, and Prophet, and King; and how, as Priest, God also made him a sacrifice for sins; and how, as Prophet, God also made him a Lawgiver to his people; and how, as King, God has also made him Judge of all the world and given him prerogatives which in the Old Testament are exclusively Jehovah's own, namely to reign till every knee bows before him and to save all who call on his name. In short, the good news was just this: that God has executed his eternal intention of glorifying his Son by exalting him as a great Savior for great sinners.

Such is the gospel which Paul was sent to preach. It is a message of some complexity, needing to be learned before it can be lived by, and understood before it can be applied. It needs, therefore, to be *taught*. Hence Paul, as a preacher of it, had to become a teacher. He saw this as part of his calling; he speaks of "the gospel, for which I was appointed a preacher . . . *and teacher*" (2 Tim 1:10-11).

And he tells us that teaching was basic to his evangelistic practice; he speaks of "him [Christ] we proclaim . . . *teaching everyone* with all wisdom" (Col 1:28). In both texts the reference to teaching is explanatory of the reference to preaching. In other words: it is by teaching that the gospel preacher fulfills his ministry. To *teach* the gospel is his first responsibility: to reduce it to its simplest essentials, to analyze it point by point, to fix its meaning by positive and negative definition, to show how each part of the message links up with the rest—and to go on explaining it till he is quite sure that his listeners have grasped it. And therefore when Paul preached the gospel, formally or informally, in the synagogue or in the streets, to Jews or to Gentiles, to a crowd or to one man, what he did was to *teach*—engaging attention, capturing interest, setting out the facts, explaining their significance, solving difficulties, answering objections, and showing how the message bears on life. Luke's regular way of describing Paul's evangelistic ministry is to say that he *disputed* (Acts 9:29), or *reasoned* (Acts 17:2, 17; 18:4; 19:8-9 [*dialegomai* rendered "argued" in the RSV]; 24:25), or *taught* (Acts 18:11; 28:31), or *persuaded* (i.e., sought to carry his hearers' judgments; Acts 18:4; 19:8, 26; 28:23; cf. 26:28). And Paul himself refers to his ministry among the Gentiles as primarily a task of instruction: "to me . . . to preach to the Gentiles the unsearchable riches of

Christ, and *to make all men see* what is the plan of the mystery" (Eph 3:8-9 RSV). Clearly, in Paul's view, his first and fundamental job as a preacher of the gospel was to communicate knowledge—to get gospel truth fixed in people's minds. To him, teaching the truth was the basic evangelistic activity; to him, therefore, the only right method of evangelism was the teaching method.

3. Paul's ultimate aim in evangelism was to convert his hearers to faith in Christ. The word "convert" is a translation of the Greek *epistrephō,* which means—and is sometimes translated—"turn." We think of conversion as a work of God, and so from one standpoint it is; but it is striking to observe that in the three New Testament passages where *epistrephō* is used transitively, of "converting" someone to God, the subject of the verb is not God, as we might have expected, but a preacher. The angel said of John the Baptist: "And he will *turn* many of the children of Israel to the Lord their God" (Lk 1:16). James says: "My brothers, if anyone among you wanders from the truth and someone *brings* him *back,* let him know that whoever *brings back* a sinner . . . will save his soul from death" (Jas 5:19-20). And Paul himself tells Agrippa how Christ had said to him: "the Gentiles—to whom I am sending you to open their eyes, so that they may turn from darkness to light and from the power of Satan to God," and how he had obeyed the heavenly vision by proclaiming to both Jews and Gentiles "that they should repent and *turn* to God" (Acts 26:17-18, 20). These passages represent the converting of others as the work of God's people, a task that they are to perform by summoning people to turn to God in repentance and faith.

When the Scriptures speak in this way of converting, and of saving too, as a task for God's people to perform, they are not, of course, calling in question the truth that, properly speaking, it is God who converts and saves. What they are saying is simply that the conversion and salvation of others should be the Christian's objective. The preacher should work to convert his congregation; the wife should work to save her unbelieving husband (1 Cor 7:16). Christians are sent to convert, and they should not allow themselves, as Christ's representatives in the world, to aim at anything less. Evangelizing, therefore, is not simply a matter of teaching, and instructing, and imparting information to the mind. There is more to it than that. Evangelizing includes the endeavor to elicit a response to the truth taught. It is communication with a view to conversion. It is a matter, not merely of informing, but also of inviting. It is an attempt to *gain* (KJV), or *win* (ESV), or *catch* our fellow men for Christ (see 1 Cor 9:19ff.; 1 Pet 3:1; Lk 5:10). Our Lord depicts it as fishermen's work (Mt 4:19; cf. 13:47).

Paul, again, is our model here. Paul, as we saw, knew himself to be sent by Christ, not only to open men's minds by teaching them the gospel (though that must come first), but also to turn them to God by exhorting and applying the truth to their lives. Accordingly, his avowed aim was not just to spread information, but to save sinners: "that by all means I might save some" (1 Cor 9:22; cf. Rom 11:14). Thus, there was in his evangelistic preaching both instruction—"in Christ God was reconciling the world to himself"—and entreaty—"We implore you on behalf of Christ, be reconciled to God" (2

Cor 5:19-20). His responsibility extended not only toward the gospel which he was charged to preach and preserve but also toward the needy people to whom he was sent to impart it and who were perishing without it (cf. Rom 1:13ff.). As an apostle of Christ, he was more than a teacher of truth; he was a shepherd of souls, sent into the world, not to lecture sinners, but to love them. For he was an apostle second and a Christian first; and, as a Christian, he was a man called to love his neighbor. This meant simply that in every situation, and by every means in his power, it was his business to seek other people's good. From this standpoint, the significance of his apostolic commission to evangelize and found churches was simply that this was the particular way in which Christ was calling him to fulfill the law of love to his neighbor. He might not, therefore, preach the gospel in a harsh, callous way, putting it before his neighbor with a contemptuous air of "there you are—take it or leave it," and excusing himself for his unconcern about people on the grounds of his faithfulness to the truth. Such conduct would be a failure of love on his part. His business was to present truth in a spirit of love, as an expression and implementation of his desire to save his hearers. The attitude which informed all Paul's evangelism was this: "I seek not what is yours but you . . . I will most gladly spend and be spent for your souls" (2 Cor 12:14-15).

And all our own evangelism must be done in the same spirit. As love to our neighbor suggests and demands that we evangelize, so the command to evangelize is a specific application of the command to love others for Christ's sake, and must be fulfilled as such.

Love made Paul warm-hearted and affectionate in his evangelism. "We were gentle among you," he reminded the Thessalonians; "being affectionately desirous of you, we were ready to share with you not only the gospel of God but also our own selves, because you had become very dear to us" (1 Thess 2:7-8). Love also made Paul considerate and adaptable in his evangelism; though he peremptorily refused to change his message to please men (cf. Gal 1:10; 2 Cor 2:17; 1 Thess 2:4), he would go to any lengths in his presentation of it to avoid giving offense and putting needless difficulties in the way of men's accepting and responding to it. "Though I am free from all," he wrote to the Corinthians, "I have made myself a slave to all, that I might win the more. To the Jews I became as a Jew, in order to win Jews; to those under the law I became as one under the law . . . that I might win those under the law. To those outside the law I became as one outside the law . . . that I might win those outside the law. To the weak I became weak, that I might win the weak. I have become all things to all men, that I might by all means save some" (1 Cor 9:19-22 RSV; cf. 10:33). Paul sought to save men; and because he sought to save them, he was not content merely to throw truth at them; but he went out of his way to get alongside them, and to start thinking with them from where they were, and to speak to them in terms that they could understand, and above all, to avoid everything that would prejudice them against the gospel and put stumbling blocks in their path. In his zeal to maintain truth, he never lost sight of the needs and claims of people. His aim and object in all his handling of the gospel, even in the heat of the polemics which contrary views evoked, was never less than to win souls, by converting those whom he saw as his neighbors, to faith in the Lord Jesus Christ.

Such was evangelism according to Paul: going out in love, as Christ's agent in the world, to teach sinners the truth of the gospel with a view to converting and saving them. If, therefore, we are engaging in this activity, in this spirit and with this aim, we are evangelizing, irrespective of the particular means by which we are doing it.

We saw earlier how wrong our thinking would go if we defined evangelism too broadly and fell into assuming that the production of converts was our personal responsibility. We would now point out that there is an opposite mistake which we must also avoid: the mistake, that is, of defining evangelism too narrowly. One way of making this mistake would be to define evangelism institutionally, in terms of holding some particular type of evangelistic meeting—a meeting, let us say, run on informal lines, at which testimonies are given, choruses are sung, and an appeal is made at the close for some outward sign of having received Christ, such as raising the hand, or standing, or walking to the front. Should we equate the church's evangelistic responsibility with the holding of such meetings, or the Christian's evangelistic responsibility with bringing unconverted people to such meetings, we should be grievously astray, as the following considerations will show.

1. In the first place, there are many ways of bringing the gospel before the unconverted in order to win them, besides

getting them to meetings of this type. There is, to start with, the way of personal evangelism, by which Andrew won Peter, and Philip won Nathanael, and Paul won Onesimus (Jn 1:40-51; Philem 10). There is the home meeting and the group Bible study. Also, and most important, there are the regular services Sunday by Sunday in local churches. Insofar as the preaching at our Sunday services is scriptural, those services will of necessity be evangelistic. It is a mistake to suppose that evangelistic sermons are a special brand of sermons, having their own peculiar style and conventions; evangelistic sermons are just scriptural sermons, the sort of sermons that a man cannot help preaching if he is preaching the Bible biblically. Proper sermons seek to expound and apply what is in the Bible. But what is in the Bible is just the whole counsel of God for man's salvation; all Scripture bears witness, in one way or another, to Christ, and all biblical themes relate to him. All proper sermons, therefore, will of necessity declare Christ in some fashion and so be more or less directly evangelistic. Some sermons, of course, will aim more narrowly and exclusively at converting sinners than do others. But you cannot present the Lord Jesus Christ as the Bible presents him, as God's answer to every problem in the sinner's relationship with himself, and not be in effect evangelistic all the time. The Lord Jesus Christ, said Robert Bolton, is "offered most freely, and without exception of any person, every Sabbath, every Sermon, either in plaine, and direct terms, or implyedly, at the least."[1] So it is, inevitably, wherever the Bible is preached biblically. And there is something

---

[1]*Instructions for a Right Comforting Afflicted Consciences*, 3rd. ed. (1640), p. 185.

terribly wrong in any church, or any man's ministry, to which
Bolton's generalization does not apply. If in our churches
"evangelistic" meetings, and "evangelistic" sermons, are
thought of as special occasions, different from the ordinary
run of things, it is a damning indictment of our normal Sunday services. So that if we should imagine that the essential
work of evangelism lies in holding meetings of the special
type described out of church hours, so to speak, that would
simply prove that we had failed to understand what our regular Sunday services are for.

2. Second, imagine a local church, or fellowship of Christians, who are giving themselves wholeheartedly to evangelism by the means mentioned above—personal work, home
meetings and gospel preaching at their ordinary services—
but have never had occasion to hold, or to join in, evangelistic
meetings of the special sort that we are considering. If we
equated the Christian duty of evangelism with running and
supporting such meetings, we should have to conclude that
this church or fellowship, because it eschewed them, was not
evangelizing at all. But that would be like arguing that you
cannot really be an Englishman unless you live at Frintonon
Sea. And it would surely be a little odd to condemn people for
not evangelizing just because they do not join in meetings of a
type of which there is no trace in the New Testament. Was no
evangelizing done, then, in New Testament times?

3. In the third place, it needs to be said that a meeting, or
service, is not necessarily evangelistic just because it includes testimonies, and choruses, and an appeal, any more
than a man is necessarily English because he wears striped

trousers and a bowler hat. The way to find out whether a particular service was evangelistic is to ask not whether an appeal for a decision was made, but what truth was taught at it. If it transpired that an insufficient gospel was preached, making the appeal for a response unintelligible to the congregation, the right of the meeting to be called evangelistic would be very doubtful.

We say these things, not to grind a polemical axe, but simply in the interests of clear thinking. It is no part of our purpose to belittle evangelistic meetings and campaigns as such. We are not suggesting that there is no place at all for special evangelistic meetings; that, in face of the rampant paganism of the modern world, would be excessively foolish. The only point we are making here is that there is a place for other forms of evangelistic action too; indeed, under certain circumstances, a prior place. Because God has used meetings, and series of meetings, of this type in the past, there is a certain surface plausibility about the idea that they constitute the normal, natural and necessary, and indeed only, pattern of evangelism for the present and the future. But this does not follow. There can be evangelism without these meetings. They are in no way essential to the practice of evangelism. Wherever, and by whatever means, the gospel is communicated with a view to conversion, there you have evangelism. Evangelism is to be defined not institutionally, in terms of the kind of meeting held, but theologically, in terms of what is taught, and for what purpose.

What principles should guide us in assessing the value of different methods of evangelism, and how much the Christian duty to evangelize really involves for us, we shall discuss at a later stage.

WHAT IS THE EVANGELISTIC MESSAGE?

We shall have to deal with this fairly summarily. In a word, the evangelistic message is the gospel of Christ, and him crucified; the message of man's sin and God's grace, of human guilt and divine forgiveness, of new birth and new life through the gift of the Holy Spirit. It is a message made up of four essential ingredients.

1. The gospel is a message about God. It tells us who he is, what his character is, what his standards are and what he requires of us, his creatures. It tells us that we owe our very existence to him, that for good or ill we are always in his hands and under his eye, and that he made us to worship and serve him, to show forth his praise and to live for his glory. These truths are the foundation of theistic religion, and until they are grasped the rest of the gospel message will seem neither cogent nor relevant. It is here, with the assertion of man's complete and constant dependence on his Creator, that the Christian story starts.

We can learn again from Paul at this point. When preaching to Jews, as at Pisidian Antioch (Acts 13:16ff.), he did not need to mention the fact that men were God's creatures; he could take this knowledge for granted, for his hearers had the Old Testament faith behind them. He could begin at once to declare Christ to them, as the fulfillment of Old Testament hopes. But when preaching to Gentiles, who knew nothing of the Old Testament, Paul had to go further back and start from the beginning. And the beginning from which Paul started in such cases was the doctrine of God's Creatorship and man's creaturehood. So when the Athenians asked him to explain what his talk of Jesus and the resurrection was all about, he spoke to them first of God the Creator, and what he made man for. "God . . . made the world. . . . [H]e himself gives to all mankind life and breath and everything. And he made . . . every nation of mankind . . . that they should seek God" (Acts 17:24-27; see also Acts 14:15ff.). This was not, as some have supposed, a piece of philosophical apologetic of a kind that Paul afterward renounced, but it was the first and basic lesson in theistic faith. The gospel starts by teaching us that we, as creatures, are absolutely dependent on God, and that he, as Creator, has an absolute claim on us. Only when we have learned this can we see what sin is, and only when we see what sin is can we understand the good news of salvation from sin. We must know what it means to call God Creator before we can grasp what it means to speak of him as Redeemer. Nothing can be achieved by talking about sin and salvation where this preliminary lesson has not in some measure been learned.

2. *The gospel is a message about* sin. It tells us how we have fallen short of God's standard; how we have become guilty, filthy and helpless in sin, and now stand under the wrath of God. It tells us that the reason why we sin continually is that we are sinners by nature, and that nothing we do, or try to do, for ourselves can put us right or bring us back into God's favor. It shows us ourselves as God sees us, and teaches us to think of ourselves as God thinks of us.

Thus it leads us to self-despair. And this also is a necessary step. Not till we have learned our need to get right with God, and our inability to do so by any effort of our own, can we come to know the Christ who saves from sin.

There is a pitfall here. Everybody's life includes things which cause dissatisfaction and shame. Everyone has a bad conscience about some things in his past, matters in which he has fallen short of the standard which he set for himself, or which was expected of him by others. The danger is that in our evangelism we should content ourselves with evoking thoughts of these things and making people feel uncomfortable about them, and then depicting Christ as the One who saves us from these elements of ourselves, without even raising the question of our relationship with God. But this is just the question that has to be raised when we speak about sin. For the very idea of sin in the Bible is of an offense against God, which disrupts a man's relationship with God. Unless we see our shortcomings in the light of the law and holiness of God, we do not see them *as sin* at all. For sin is not a social concept; it is a theological concept. Though sin is committed by man, and many sins are against society, sin cannot be defined in terms of either man or society. We never know what sin really is till we have learned to think of it in terms of God, and to measure it, not by human standards, but by the yardstick of his total demand on our lives.

What we have to grasp, then, is that the bad conscience of the natural man is not at all the same thing as conviction of sin. It does not, therefore, follow that a man is convicted of sin when he is distressed about his weaknesses and the wrong things he has done. It is not conviction of sin just to feel miserable about yourself and your failures and your inadequacy to meet life's demands. Nor would it be saving faith if a man in that condition called on the Lord Jesus Christ just to soothe him, cheer him up and make him feel confident again. Nor should we be preaching the gospel (though we might imagine we were) if all that we did was to present Christ in terms of a human's felt wants. ("Are you happy? Are you satisfied? Do you want peace of mind? Do you feel that you have failed? Are you fed up with yourself? Do you want a friend? Then come to Christ; he will meet your every need"—as if the Lord Jesus Christ were to be thought of as a fairy godmother, or a super-psychiatrist.) No; we have to go deeper than this. To preach sin means not to make capital out of people's felt frailties (the brainwasher's trick), but to measure their lives by the holy law of God. To be convicted of sin means not just to feel that one is an all-around flop, but to realize that one has offended God, flouted his authority, defied him, gone against him and put oneself in the wrong with him. To preach Christ means to set him forth as the One who, through his cross, sets men right with God again. To put faith in Christ means relying on him, and him alone, to restore us to God's fellowship and favor.

It is indeed true that the real Christ, the Christ of the Bible, who offers himself to us as Savior from sin and Advocate with God, does in fact give peace and joy and moral strength and the privilege of his own friendship to those who trust him. But the Christ who is depicted and desired merely to make the lot of life's casualties easier by supplying them with aids and comforts is not the real Christ, but a misrepresented and misconceived Christ—in effect, an imaginary Christ. And if we taught people to look to an imaginary Christ, we should have no grounds for expecting that they would find real salvation. We must be on our guard, therefore, against equating a natural bad conscience and sense of wretchedness with spiritual conviction of sin, and so omitting in our evangelism to sinners the basic truth about their condition—namely, that their sin has alienated them from God and exposed them to his condemnation, hostility and wrath, so that their first need is for a restored relationship with him.

It may be asked: what are the signs of true conviction of sin, as distinct from the mere smart of a natural bad conscience, or the mere disgust at life which any disillusioned person may feel?

The signs seem to be three in number.

(1) *Conviction of sin is essentially an awareness of a wrong relationship with God.* It is not just a wrong relationship with one's neighbor, or one's own conscience and ideals for oneself, but with one's Maker, the God in whose hand one's breath is and on whom one depends for existence every moment. To define conviction of sin as a sense of need, without qualification, would not be enough; it is not any sense of need, but a sense of a particular need—a need, namely, for restoration of fellowship with God. It is the realization that, as one stands at present, one is in a relationship with God that spells only rejection, retribution, wrath and pain for the present and the future; and a realization that this is an intol-

erable relationship to remain in, and therefore a desire that, at whatever cost and on whatever terms, it might be changed. Conviction of sin may center on the sense of one's guilt before God, or one's uncleanness in his sight, or one's rebellion against him, or one's alienation and estrangement from him; but always it is a sense of the need to get right, not simply with oneself or other people, but with God.

(2) *Conviction of sin always includes conviction of sins.* It involves a sense of guilt for particular wrongs done in the sight of God, from which one needs to turn and be rid of them if one is ever to be right with God. Thus, Isaiah was convicted specifically of sins of speech (Is 6:5) and Zacchaeus of sins of extortion (Lk 19:8).

(3) *Conviction of sin always includes conviction of sinfulness.* Sinfulness is a sense of one's complete corruption and perversity in God's sight, and one's consequent need of what Ezekiel called a "new heart" (Ezek 36:26), and in our Lord, a new birth (Jn 3:3-7, i.e., a moral re-creation). Thus, the author of Psalm 51—traditionally identified with David, convicted of his sin with Bathsheba—confesses not only particular transgressions (verses 1-4) but also the depravity of his nature (verses 5-6), and seeks cleansing from the guilt and defilement of both (verses 7-10). Indeed, perhaps the shortest way to tell whether a person is convicted of sin or not is to take him through Psalm 51, and see whether his heart is in fact speaking anything like the language of the psalmist.

3. The gospel is a message about **Christ**. Christ is the Son of God incarnate; Christ is the Lamb of God, who died for sin; Christ is the risen Lord; Christ is the perfect Savior.

Two points need to be made about the declaring of this part of the message.

(1) *We must not present the Person of Christ apart from his saving work.* It is sometimes said that it is the presentation of Christ's Person, rather than of doctrines about him, that draws sinners to his feet. It is true that it is the living Christ who saves, and that a theory of the atonement, however orthodox, is no substitute. When this remark is made, however, what is usually being suggested is that doctrinal instruction is dispensable in evangelistic preaching, and that all the evangelist need do is paint a vivid word-picture of the Man of Galilee who went about doing good and then assure the hearers that this Jesus is still alive to help them in their troubles. But such a message could hardly be called the gospel. It would, in reality, be a mere conundrum, serving only to mystify. Who was this Jesus? we should ask; and what is his position now? Such preaching would raise these questions while concealing the answers. And thus it would completely baffle the thoughtful listener.

For the truth is that you cannot make sense of the historic figure of Jesus till you know about the *incarnation*—that this Jesus was in fact God the Son, made man to save sinners according to his Father's eternal purpose. Nor can you make sense of his life till you know about the *atonement*—that he lived as man so that he might die as man for men, and that his passion, his judicial murder, was really his saving action of bearing away the world's sins. Nor can you tell on what terms to approach him now till you know about the *resurrection, ascension* and *heavenly session*—that Jesus has been raised, and enthroned, and made King, and lives to save to the uttermost all who acknowledge his lordship. These doctrines, to mention no others, are essential to the gospel. Without them, there is no gospel, only a puzzle story about a man named Jesus. To oppose the teaching of doctrines about Christ to the presenting of his Person is, therefore, to put asunder two things which God has joined. It is really very perverse indeed; for the whole purpose of teaching these doctrines in evangelism is to throw light on the Person of the Lord Jesus Christ, and to make clear to our hearers just who it is that we want them to meet. When, in ordinary social life, we want people to know who it is that we are introducing them to, we tell them something about him and what he has done; and so it is here. The apostles themselves preached these doctrines in order to preach Christ, as the New Testament shows. In fact, without these doctrines you would have no gospel to preach at all. But there is a second and complementary point.

(2) *We must not present the saving work of Christ apart from his Person.* Evangelistic preachers and personal workers have sometimes been known to make this mistake. In their concern to focus attention on the atoning death of Christ, as the sole sufficient ground on which sinners may be accepted with God, they have expounded the summons to saving faith in these terms: "Believe that Christ died for your sins." The effect of this exposition is to represent the saving work of Christ in the past, dissociated from his Person in the present, as the whole object of our trust. But it is not biblical thus to isolate the work from the Worker. Nowhere in the New

Testament is the call to believe expressed in such terms. What the New Testament calls for is faith in (*en*) or into (*eis*) or upon (*epi*) Christ himself—the placing of our trust in the living Savior, who died for sins. The object of saving faith is thus not, strictly speaking, the atonement, but the Lord Jesus Christ, who made atonement. We must not, in presenting the gospel, isolate the cross and its benefits from the Christ whose cross it was. For the persons to whom the benefits of Christ's death belong are just those who trust his Person, and believe not upon his saving death simply, but upon *him*, the living Savior. "Believe in *the Lord Jesus*, and you will be saved" (Acts 16:31), said Paul. "Come to *me* . . . and *I* will give you rest" (Mt 11:28), said our Lord.

This being so, one thing becomes clear straight away: namely, that the question about the extent of the atonement, which is being much agitated in some quarters, has no bearing on the content of the evangelistic message at this particular point. I do not propose to discuss this question now; I have done that elsewhere.[2] I am not at present asking you whether you think it is true to say that Christ died in order to save every single human being—past, present and fu-

---

[2]In my introduction to the 1959 reprint of *The Death of Death in the Death of Christ* by John Owen. Owen's book is a classical discussion of the complex questions that the controversy about "limited atonement" involves. The central issue does not concern the value of the atonement, considered in itself, nor the availability of Christ to those who would trust him as their Savior. All agree that no limit can be set to the intrinsic worth of Christ's death, and that Christ never casts out those who come to him. The cleavage is over the question, whether the intention of the Father and the Son in the great transaction of Calvary was to save any more than actually are saved. There is no room here to open up this elaborate question; and in any case, nothing in the text depends one way or the other on the answer that one gives to it.

ture—or not. Nor am I at present inviting you to make up your mind on this question, if you have not done so already. All I want to say here is that even if you think the above assertion is true, your presentation of Christ in evangelism ought not differ from that of the man who thinks it false.

What I mean is this. It is obvious that if a preacher thought that the statement "Christ died for every one of you," made to any congregation, would be unverifiable, and probably not true, he would take care not to make it in his gospel preaching. You do not find such statements in the sermons of, for instance, George Whitefield or Charles Spurgeon. But now, my point is that, even if a man thinks that this statement would be true if he made it, it is not a thing that he ever needs to say, or ever has reason to say, when preaching the gospel. For preaching the gospel, as we have just seen, means inviting sinners to come to Jesus Christ, the living Savior, who, by virtue of his atoning death, is able to forgive and save all those who put their trust in him. What has to be said about the cross when preaching the gospel is simply that Christ's death is the ground on which Christ's forgiveness is given. And this is all that has to be said. The question of the designed extent of the atonement does not come into the story at all.

The fact is that the New Testament never calls on any man to repent on the ground that Christ died specifically and particularly for him. The basis on which the New Testament invites sinners to put faith in Christ is simply that they need him, and that he offers himself to them, and that those who receive him are promised all the benefits that his death secured for his people. What is universal and all-inclusive in the New Testament is the invitation to faith and the promise of salvation to all who believe (see Mt 11:28ff.; 22:9; Lk 2:10-11; 12:8; Jn 1:12; 3:14ff.; 6:40, 54; 7:37; 11:26; 12:46; Acts 2:21; 10:43; 13:39; Rom 1:16; 3:22; 9:33; 10:4ff.; Gal 3:22; Tit 2:11; Rev 22:17; cf. Is 4:1).

Our task in evangelism is to reproduce as faithfully as possible the New Testament emphasis. To go beyond the New Testament, or to distort its viewpoint or shift its stress, is always wrong. And therefore—if we may at this point speak in the words of James Denney—"we do not think of separating [Christ's] work from him who achieved it. The New Testament knows only of a living Christ, and all apostolic preaching of the gospel holds up the living Christ to men. But the living Christ is Christ who died, and he is never preached apart from his death, and from its reconciling power. It is *the living Christ, with the virtue of his reconciling death in him,* who is the burden of the apostolic message. . . . The task of the evangelist is to preach Christ . . . *in his character as the Crucified.*"[3] The gospel is not "believe that Christ died for everybody's sins, and therefore for yours," any more than it is "believe that Christ died only for certain people's sins, and so perhaps not for yours." The gospel is "believe on the Lord Jesus Christ, who died for sins, and now offers you himself as your Savior." This is the message which we are to take to the world. We have no business to ask them to put faith in any view of the extent of the atonement; our job is to point them to the living Christ, and summon them to trust in him.

It was because they had both grasped this that John Wesley

---

[3]*The Christian Doctrine of Reconciliation,* p. 287; my italics.

and George Whitefield could regard each other as brothers in evangelism, though they differed on the extent of the atonement. For their views on this subject did not enter into their gospel preaching. Both were content to preach the gospel just as it stands in Scripture: that is, to proclaim "the living Christ, with the virtue of his reconciling death in him," to offer him to sinners, and to invite the lost to come to him and so find life. This brings us to the final ingredient in the gospel message.

4. The gospel is a summons to **faith and repentance**. All who hear the gospel are summoned by God to repent and believe. "He [God] commands all people everywhere to *repent,*" Paul told the Athenians (Acts 17:30). When asked by his hearers what they should do in order to "be doing the works of God," our Lord replied: "This is the work of God, that you *believe* in him whom he has sent" (Jn 6:29). And in 1 John 3:23 we read: "This is his *commandment,* that we believe in the name of his Son Jesus Christ." Repentance and faith are rendered matters of duty by God's direct command, and hence impenitence and unbelief are singled out in the New Testament as most grievous sins (cf. Lk 13:3, 5; 2 Thess 2:11-12). With these universal commands, as we indicated above, go universal promises of salvation to all who obey them: "*Everyone who believes* in him receives forgiveness of sins through his name" (Acts 10:43), "Let the one *who desires* take the water of life without price" (Rev 22:17), "God so loved the world, that he gave his only Son, that *whoever believes* in him should not perish but have eternal life" (Jn 3:16). These words are promises to which God will stand as long as time shall last.

It needs to be said that faith is not a mere optimistic feeling, any more than repentance is a mere regretful or remorseful feeling. Faith and repentance are both acts, and acts of the whole man. Faith is more than just credence; faith is essentially the casting and resting of oneself and one's confidence on the promises of mercy, which Christ has given to sinners, and on the Christ who gave those promises. Equally, repentance is more than just sorrow for the past; repentance is a change of mind and heart, a new life of denying self and serving the Savior as king in self's place. Mere credence without trusting, and mere remorse without turning, do not save. "Even the demons believe—and shudder!" (Jas 2:19). "Worldly grief produces death" (2 Cor 7:10).

Two further points need to be made also.

(1) *The demand is for faith as well as repentance.* It is not enough to resolve to turn from sin, and give up evil habits, and try to put Christ's teaching into practice by being religious and doing all possible good to others. Aspiration, resolution, morality and religiosity are no substitutes for faith. Martin Luther and John Wesley had all these long before they had faith. If there is to be faith, however, there must be a foundation of knowledge: a man must know of Christ, of his cross and of his promises before saving faith becomes a possibility for him. In our presentation of the gospel, therefore, we need to stress these things, in order to lead sinners to abandon all confidence in themselves and to trust wholly in Christ and the power of his redeeming blood to give them acceptance with God. For nothing less than this is faith.

(2) *The demand is for repentance as well as faith.* It is not enough to believe that only through Christ and his death are

sinners justified and accepted, and that one's own record is sufficient to bring down God's condemning sentence twenty times over, and that, apart from Christ, one has no hope. Knowledge of the gospel, and orthodox belief of it, is no substitute for repentance. If there is to be repentance, however, there must, again, be a foundation of knowledge. A man must know that, in the words of the first of Luther's Ninety-Five Theses, "when our Lord and Master, Jesus Christ, said 'Repent,' he called for the entire life of believers to be one of repentance," and he must also know what repentance involves. More than once, Christ deliberately called attention to the radical break with the past that repentance involves. "If anyone would come after me, let him *deny himself* and take up his cross daily and follow me. . . . [W]hoever *loses his life for my sake* [but only he] will save it" (Lk 9:23-24). "If anyone comes to me and *does not hate* his own father and mother and wife and children and brothers and sisters, yes, and even his own life [i.e., put them all decisively second in his esteem], *he cannot be my disciple*" (Lk 14:26).

"Any one of you who does not renounce all that he has cannot be my disciple." The repentance that Christ requires of his people consists in a settled refusal to set any limit to the claims which he may make on their lives. Our Lord knew—who better?—how costly his followers would find it to maintain this refusal, and let him have his way with them all the time, and therefore he wished them to face out and think through the implications of discipleship before committing themselves. He did not desire to make disciples under false pretenses. He had no interest in gathering vast crowds of professed adherents who would melt away as soon as they found out what following him actually demanded of them. In our own presentation of Christ's gospel, therefore, we need to lay a similar stress on the cost of following Christ, and make sinners face it soberly before we urge them to respond to the message of free forgiveness. In common honesty, we must not conceal the fact that free forgiveness, in one sense, will cost everything; or else our evangelizing becomes a sort of confidence trick. And where there is no clear knowledge, and hence no realistic recognition of the real claims that Christ makes, there can be no repentance, and therefore no salvation. Such is the evangelistic message that we are sent to make known.

WHAT IS THE MOTIVE FOR EVANGELIZING?

There are, in fact, two motives that should spur us constantly to evangelize. The first is love of God and concern for his glory; the second is love of man and concern for his welfare.

1. The *first* motive is primary and fundamental. The chief end of man is to glorify God. The biblical rule of life is "do all to the glory of God" (1 Cor 10:31). Men glorify God by obeying his word and fulfilling his revealed will. Similarly, the first and great commandment is "You shall love the Lord your God" (Mt 22:37). We show love to the Father and the Son, who have so richly loved us, by keeping their commandments.

"Whoever has my commandments and keeps them, he it is who loves me," said our Lord (Jn 14:21). "This is the love of God," wrote John, "that we keep his commandments" (1 Jn 5:3). Now, evangelism is one of the activities that the Father and the Son have commanded. "This gospel of the kingdom," Christ tells us, "will [according to Mark, "must"] be proclaimed throughout the whole world as a testimony" (Mt 24:14; Mk 13:10). And before his ascension Christ charged his disciples in the following categorical terms: "Go . . . and make disciples of all nations." To this command he added at once a comprehensive promise: "And lo, I am with you always, to the close of the age" (Mt 28:19-20 RSV). The comprehensiveness of this promise shows us how wide is the application of the command to which it is appended. The phrase "to the close of the age" makes it clear that the "you" to whom the promise was given was not solely and exclusively the eleven disciples; this promise extends to the whole Christian church throughout history, the entire community of which the eleven were, so to speak, founding members. It is, therefore, a promise for us no less than for them, and a promise of great comfort too. But if the promise extends to us, then the commission with which it is linked must extend to us also. The promise was given to encourage the eleven, lest they be overwhelmed at the size and difficulty of the task of world evangelism that Christ was laying on them. If it is our privilege to appropriate the promise, then it is also our responsibility to accept the commission. The task laid on the eleven is the church's constant task. And if it is the church's task in general, then it is your task and my task in particular. If, therefore, we love God and are concerned to glorify him, we must obey his command to evangelize.

There is a further strand to this thought. We glorify God by evangelizing, not only because evangelizing is an act of obedience, but also because in evangelism we tell the world what great things God has done for the salvation of sinners. God is glorified when his mighty works of grace are made known. The psalmist exhorts us to "tell of his salvation from day to day. / Declare his glory among the nations, / his marvelous works among all the peoples!" (Ps 96:2-3). For a Christian to talk to the unconverted about the Lord Jesus Christ and his saving power is in itself honoring and glorifying to God.

2. The *second* motive that should prompt us to assiduous evangelism is love of our neighbor, and the desire to see our fellow humans saved. The wish to win the lost for Christ should be, and indeed is, the natural, spontaneous outflow of love in the heart of everyone who has been born again. Our Lord confirms the Old Testament demand that we should love our neighbor as ourselves (Mk 12:31; Lk 10:27-28). "As we have opportunity," writes Paul, "let us do good to everyone" (Gal 6:10). What greater need has any man than the need to know Christ? What greater good can we do to any man than to set before him the knowledge of Christ? Insofar as we really love our neighbor as ourselves, we shall of necessity want him to enjoy the salvation which is so precious to us. This, indeed, should not be a thing that we need to think about, let alone argue about. The impulse to evangelize should spring up spontaneously in us as we see our neighbor's need of Christ.

Who is my neighbor? When the lawyer, confronted with the demand of love for one's neighbor, asked our Lord this question, Christ replied by telling the story of the Good Samaritan (Lk 10:29-37). What that story teaches is simply this: that any fellow human being whom you meet who is in need is your neighbor; God has put him there so that you may help him; and your business is to show yourself neighbor to him by doing all that you can to meet his need, whatever it may be. "You go, and do likewise," said our Lord to the lawyer. He says the same to us. And the principle applies to all forms of need, spiritual no less than material. So that when we find ourselves in contact with men and women who are without Christ and so face spiritual death, we are to look on them as our neighbors in this sense and ask ourselves what we can do to make Christ known to them.

May I stress again: if we ourselves have known anything of the love of Christ for us, and if our hearts have felt any measure of gratitude for the grace that has saved us from death and hell, then this attitude of compassion and care for our spiritually needy fellow men ought to come naturally and spontaneously to us. It was in connection with aggressive evangelism that Paul declared that "the love of Christ controls us" (2 Cor 5:14). It is a tragic and ugly thing when Christians lack desire, and are actually reluctant, to share the precious knowledge that they have with others whose need of it is just as great as their own. It was natural for Andrew, when he found the Messiah, to go off and tell his brother Simon, and for Philip to hurry to break the good news to his friend Nathanael (Jn 1:40ff.). They did not need to be told to do this; they did it naturally and spontaneously, just as one would naturally and spontaneously share with one's family and friends any other piece of news that vitally affected them. There is something very wrong with us if we do not ourselves find it natural to act in this way: let us be quite clear about that. It is a great privilege to evangelize; it is a wonderful thing to be able to tell others of the love of Christ, knowing that there is nothing that they need more urgently to know, and no knowledge in the world that can do them so much good. We should not, therefore, be reluctant and backward to evangelize on the personal and individual level. We should be glad and happy to do it. We should not look for excuses for wriggling out of our obligation when occasion offers to talk to others about the Lord Jesus Christ. If we find ourselves shrinking from this responsibility and trying to evade it, we need to face ourselves with the fact that in this we are yielding to sin and Satan. If (as is usual) it is the fear of being thought odd and ridiculous, or of losing popularity in certain circles, that holds us back, we need to ask ourselves in the presence of God: Ought these things to stop us loving our neighbor? If it is a false shame, which is not shame at all but pride in disguise, that keeps our tongue from Christian witness when we are with other people. We need to press on our conscience this question: Which matters more—our reputation or their salvation? We cannot be complacent about this gangrene of conceit and cowardice when we weigh up our lives in the presence of God. What we need to do is to ask for grace to be truly ashamed of ourselves, and to pray that we may so overflow in love for God that we will overflow in love for our fellow men, and so find it an easy and natural and joyful thing to share with them the good news of Christ.

By now, I hope, it is becoming clear to us how we should

regard our evangelistic responsibility. Evangelism is not the only task that our Lord has given us, nor is it a task that we are all called to discharge in the same way. We are not all called to be preachers; we are not all given equal opportunities or comparable abilities for personal dealing with men and women who need Christ. But we all have some evangelistic responsibility which we cannot shirk without failing in love both to our God and to our neighbor. To start with, we all can and should be praying for the salvation of unconverted people, particularly in our families, and among our friends and everyday associates. And then we must learn to see what possibilities of evangelism our everyday situation holds, and to be enterprising in our use of them. It is the nature of love to be enterprising. If you love someone, you are constantly trying to think out what is the best you can do for him and how best you can please him, and it is your pleasure to give him pleasure by the things you devise for him. If, then, we love God—Father, Son and Spirit—for all that they have done for us, we shall muster all our initiative and enterprise to make the most that we can of every situation for their glory—and one chief way of doing this is to seek out ways and means of spreading the gospel, and obeying the divine command to make disciples everywhere. Similarly, if we love our neighbor, we shall muster all our initiative and enterprise to find ways and means of doing him good. And one chief way of doing him good is to share with him our knowledge of Christ. Thus, if we love God and our neighbor, we shall evangelize, and we shall be enterprising in our evangelism. We shall not ask with reluctance how much we have to do in this realm, as if evangelizing were a distasteful and burdensome task. We shall not inquire anxiously after the minimum outlay of effort in evangelism that will satisfy God. But we shall ask eagerly, and pray earnestly to be shown, just how much it is in our power to do to spread the knowledge of Christ among men; and once we see what the possibilities are, we shall give ourselves wholeheartedly to the task.

One further point must be added, however, lest what we have said be misapplied. It must never be forgotten that the enterprise required of us in evangelism is the enterprise of love: an enterprise that springs from a genuine interest in those whom we seek to win, and a genuine care for their well-being, and expresses itself in a genuine respect for them and a genuine friendliness toward them. One sometimes meets a scalp-hunting zeal in evangelism, both in the pulpit and on the personal level, which is both discreditable and alarming. It is discreditable, because it reflects, not love and care nor the desire to be of help, but arrogance and conceit and pleasure in having power over the lives of others. It is alarming, because it finds expression in a ferocious psychological pummeling of the poor victim, which may do great damage to sensitive and impressionable souls. But if love prompts and rules our evangelistic work, we shall approach other people in a different spirit. If we truly care for them, and if our hearts truly love and fear God, then we shall seek to present Christ to them in a way that is both honoring to God and respectful to them. We shall not try to violate their personalities, or exploit their weaknesses, or ride roughshod over their feelings. What we shall be trying to do, rather, is to show them the reality of our friendship and concern by sharing with them our most valuable possession. And this spirit of friendship and concern will shine through all that we say to them, whether in the pulpit or in private, however drastic and shattering the truths that we tell them may be.

There is a famous old book on personal evangelism by C. G. Trumbull, entitled *Taking Men Alive*. In the third chapter of that book, the author tells us of the rule that his father, H. C. Trumbull, made for himself in this matter. It was as follows: "Whenever I am justified in choosing my subject of conversation with another, the theme of themes [Christ] shall have prominence between us, so that I may learn of his need, and, if possible, meet it." The key words here are: *"whenever I am justified in choosing my subject of conversation with another."* They remind us, first, that personal evangelism, like all our dealings with our fellow men, should be courteous. And they remind us, second, that personal evangelism needs normally to be founded on friendship. You are not usually justified in choosing the subject of conversation with another till you have already begun to give yourself to him in friendship and established a relationship with him in which he feels that you respect him, are interested in him, and are treating him as a human being and not just as some kind of "case." With some people, you may establish such a relationship in five minutes, whereas with others it may take months. But the principle remains the same. The right to talk intimately to another person about the Lord Jesus Christ has to be earned, and you earn it by convincing him that you are his friend, and that you really care about him. And therefore the indiscriminate buttonholing, the intrusive barging in to the privacy of other people's souls, the thick-skinned insistence on expounding the things of God to reluctant strangers who are longing to get away—these modes of behavior, in which strong and loquacious personalities have sometimes indulged in the name of personal evangelism, should be written off as a travesty of personal evangelism. *Impersonal* evangelism would be a better name for them! In fact, rudeness of this sort dishonors God; moreover, it creates resentment and prejudices people against the Christ whose professed followers act so objectionably. The truth is that real personal evangelism is very costly, just because it demands of us a really personal relationship with the other person. We have to give ourselves in honest friendship to people, if ever our relationship with them is to reach the point at which we are justified in choosing to talk to them about Christ and in speaking to them about their own spiritual needs—without being either discourteous or offensive. If you wish to do personal evangelism, then—and I hope you do; you ought to—pray for the gift of friendship. A genuine friendliness is in any case a prime mark of the man who is learning to love his neighbor as himself.

BY WHAT MEANS AND METHODS SHOULD EVANGELISM BE PRACTICED?

There is today a controversy in some evangelical circles about evangelistic methods. Some are criticizing, and others are defending, the type of evangelistic meeting that has been a standard feature of English and American evangelical life for almost a century. Meetings of this type are well known, for they are very characteristic. They are deliberately made brisk and bright, in the hope that people who have little interest in the Christian message, and who may never have been inside a Christian church, may nevertheless find them an attraction. Everything is accordingly planned to create an atmosphere of warmth, good humor and happiness. The meeting normally includes a good deal of music—choir items, solo items, choruses and rousing hymns, heartily sung. Heavy emphasis is laid on the realities of Christian experience, both by the choice of hymns and by the use of testimonies. The meeting leads up to an appeal for decision, followed by an after-meeting or a time of personal counseling for the further instruction of those who have made, or wish to make, a decision in response to the appeal.

The main criticisms that are made of such meetings—whether they are wholly justified we would not venture to say—are as follows. Their breezy slickness (it is said) makes for irreverence. The attempt to give them "entertainment value" tends to lessen the sense of God's majesty, to banish the spirit of worship and to cheapen men's thoughts of their Creator; moreover, it is the worst possible preparation of the potential converts for the regular Sunday services in the churches which they will in due course join. The seemingly inevitable glamorizing of Christian experience in the testimonies is pastorally irresponsible and gives a falsely romanticized impression of what being a Christian is like. This, together with the tendency to indulge in long, drawn-out wheedling for decisions and the deliberate use of luscious music to stir sentiment, tends to produce "conversions" which are simply psychological and emotional upheavals, and not the fruit of spiritual conviction and renewal at all. The occasional character of the meetings makes it inevitable that appeals for decision will often be made on the basis of inadequate instruction as to what the decision involves and will cost, and such appeals are no better than a confidence trick. The desire to justify the meetings by reaping a crop of converts may prompt the preacher and the counselors to try and force people through the motions of decision prematurely, before they have grasped what it is really all about, and converts produced in this way tend to prove at best stunted and at worst spurious and, in the event, gospel-hardened. The way ahead in evangelism, it is said, is to break completely with this pattern of evangelistic action, and to develop a new pattern (or, rather, restore the old one which existed before this type of meeting became standard), in which the evangelizing unit is the local church rather than a group or cross-section of churches. Then the evangelistic meeting finds its place among the local church's services—a pattern, indeed, in which the local church's services function continually as its evangelistic meetings.

The usual reply is that, while the things stigmatized are certainly real abuses, evangelistic meetings of the standard pattern can be, and frequently are, run in a way that avoids them. Such meetings, it is said, have proved their usefulness in the past; experience shows that God uses them still; and there seems to be no sufficient reason for abandoning them. It is argued that, while so many churches in each major denomination are failing in their evangelistic responsibility, these meetings may well be the only opportunity for presenting the gospel to vast multitudes of our fellow men and women. The way ahead, it is maintained, is not to abolish them but to reform them where abuses exist.

The debate continues. No doubt it will remain with us for some time to come. What I want to do here is not to go into this controversy but to go behind it. I want to isolate the key principle that should guide us in our assessment both of these and any other methods of evangelism that may be practiced or proposed.

What is this key principle? The following line of thought will make it clear.

Evangelism, as we have seen, is an act of communication with a view to conversion. In the last analysis, therefore, there is only one *means* of evangelism: namely, the gospel of Christ, explained and applied. Faith and repentance, the two complementary elements of which conversion consists, occur as a response to the gospel. "Faith comes from hearing," Paul tells us, "and hearing through the word of Christ" (Rom 10:17)—or, as The New English Bible expands the verse, "faith is awakened by the message, and the message that awakens it comes through the word of Christ."

Again, in the last analysis, there is only one *agent* of evangelism: namely, the Lord Jesus Christ. It is Christ himself who through his Holy Spirit enables his servants to explain the gospel truly and apply it powerfully and effectively; just as it is Christ himself who through his Holy Spirit opens people's minds (Lk 24:25) and hearts (Acts 16:14) to receive the gospel, and so draws them savingly to himself (Jn 12:32).

Paul speaks of his achievements as an evangelist as "what *Christ has wrought through me* to win obedience from the Gentiles, by word and deed . . . *by the power of the Holy Spirit*" (Rom 15:18-19 RSV). Since Augustine, the point has often been made that Christ is the true minister of the gospel sacraments, and the human celebrant acts merely as his hand. We need to remember the equally basic truth that Christ is the true minister of the gospel word, and the human preacher or witness acts merely as his mouth.

So, in the last analysis, there is only one *method* of evangelism: namely, the faithful explanation and application of the gospel message. From which it follows—and this is the key principle which we are seeking—that the test for any proposed strategy, technique or style of evangelistic action must be this: will it in fact serve the word? Is it calculated to be a means of explaining the gospel truly and fully and applying it deeply and exactly? To the extent to which it is so calculated, it is lawful and right; to the extent to which it tends to overlay and obscure the realities of the message, and to blunt the edge of their application, it is ungodly and wrong.

Let us work this out. It means that we need to bring under review all our evangelistic plans and practices—our missions, rallies and campaigns; our sermons, talks and testimonies; our big meetings, our little meetings and our presentation of the gospel in personal dealing; the tracts that we give, the books that we lend, the letters that we write—and to ask about each of them questions such as the following:

Is this way of presenting Christ calculated to impress on people that the gospel is *a word from God*? Is it calculated to divert their attention from human and all things merely human to God and his truth? Or is its tendency rather to distract attention from the Author and authority of the message to the person and performance of the messenger? Does it make the gospel sound like a human idea, a preacher's plaything, or like a divine revelation, before which the human messenger himself stands in awe? Does this way of presenting Christ savor of human cleverness and showmanship? Does it tend thereby to exalt man? Or does it embody rather the straightforward, unaffected simplicity of the messenger whose sole concern is to deliver his message, and who has no wish to call attention to himself, and who desires so far as he can to blot himself out and hide, as it were, behind his message, fearing nothing so much as that men should admire and applaud him when they ought to be bowing down and humbling themselves before the mighty Lord whom he represents?

Again: is this way of presenting Christ calculated to promote, or impede, the work of the word in men's *minds*? Is it going to clarify the meaning of the message or leave it enigmatic and obscure, locked up in pious jargon and oracular formulae? Is it going to make people think, and think hard, and think hard about God, and about themselves in relation to God? Or will it tend to stifle thought by playing exclusively on the emotions? Is it calculated to stir the mind or put it to sleep? Is this way of presenting Christ an attempt to move men by the force of feeling or of truth? Not, of course, that there is anything wrong with emotion; it is strange for a person to be converted without emotion; what is wrong is the sort of appeal to emotion, and playing on emotion, which harrows people's feelings as a substitute for instructing their minds.

Again: we have to ask, is this way of presenting Christ calculated to convey to people the *doctrine* of the gospel, and not just part of it but the whole of it—the truth about our Creator and his claims, and about ourselves as guilty, lost and helpless sinners, needing to be born again, and about the Son of God who became man, died for sins and lives to forgive sinners and bring them to God? Or is it likely to be deficient here, deal in half-truths and leave people with an incomplete understanding of these things, hurrying them on to the demand for faith and repentance without having made it clear just what they need to repent of or what they ought to believe?

Again: we have to ask, is this way of presenting Christ calculated to convey to people the *application* of the gospel, and not just part of it but the whole of it—the summons to see and know oneself as God sees and knows one, that is, as a sinful creature, and to face the breadth and depth of the need into which a wrong relationship with God has brought one and to face too the cost and consequences of turning to receive Christ as Savior and Lord? Or is it likely to be deficient here, and to gloss over some of this, and to give an inadequate, distorted impression of what the gospel requires? Will it, for instance, leave people unaware that they have any immediate obligation to respond to Christ at all? Or will it leave them supposing that all they have to do is to trust Christ as a sin-bearer, not realizing that they must also deny themselves and enthrone him as their Lord (the error which we might call only-believism)? Or will it leave them imagining that the whole of what they have to do is to consecrate themselves to Christ as their Master, not realizing that they must also receive him as their Savior (the error which we might call good-resolutionism)? We need to remember here that spiritually it is even more dangerous for a man whose conscience is roused to make a misconceived response to the gospel and take up with a defective religious practice than for him to make no response at all. If you turn a publican into a Pharisee, you make his condition worse, not better.

Again: we have to ask, is this way of presenting Christ calculated to convey gospel truth in a manner that is appropriately *serious*? Is it calculated to make people feel that they are indeed facing a matter of life and death? Is it calculated to make them see and feel the greatness of God, and the greatness of their sin and need, and the greatness of the grace of Christ? Is it calculated to make them aware of the awful majesty and holiness of God? Will it help them to realize that it is a fearful thing to fall into his hands? Or is this way of presenting Christ so light and casual and cozy and jolly as to make it hard for the hearers to feel that the gospel is a matter of any consequence, save as a pick-me-up for life's misfits? It is a gross insult to God, and a real disservice to men, to cheapen and trivialize the gospel by one's presentation of it. Not that we should put on an affected solemnity when speaking of spiritual things; there is nothing more essentially frivolous than a mock seriousness, and nothing more likely to make hypocrites out of our hearers. What is needed is this: that we, who would speak for Christ, should pray constantly that God will put and keep in our hearts a sense of his greatness and glory, of the joy of fellowship with him, and of the dreadfulness of spending time and eternity without him; and then that God will enable us to speak honestly, straightforwardly and just as we feel about these matters. Then we shall be really natural in presenting the gospel—and really serious too.

It is by asking questions of this sort that we must test and, where necessary, reform our evangelistic methods. The principle is that the best method of evangelism is the one which serves the gospel most completely. It is the one which bears the clearest witness to the divine origin of the message and to the life-and-death character of the issues which it raises. It is the one which makes possible the most full and thorough explanation of the good news of Christ and his cross, and the most exacting and searching application of it. It is the one which most effectively engages the minds of those to whom witness is borne and makes them most vividly aware that the gospel is God's word, addressed personally to them in their own situation. What that best method is in each case, you and I have to find out for ourselves. It is in the light of this principle that all debates about evangelistic methods must be decided. For the present, we leave the matter there.

4

DIVINE SOVEREIGNTY
AND EVANGELISM

We start this final section by summing up what we have learned so far about evangelism.

Evangelism, we have learned, is a task appointed to all God's people everywhere. It is the task of communicating a message from the Creator to rebel mankind. The message begins with information and ends with an invitation. The information concerns God's work of making his Son a perfect Savior for sinners. The invitation is God's summons to mankind generally to come to the Savior and find life. God commands all men everywhere to repent, and promises forgiveness and restoration to all who do. The Christian is sent into the world as God's herald and Christ's ambassador, to broadcast this message as widely as he can. This is both his duty (because God commands it, and love to our neighbor requires it) and his privilege (because it is a great thing to speak for God, and to take our neighbor the remedy—the only remedy—that can save him from the terrors of spiritual death). Our job, then, is to go to our fellow men and tell them the gospel of Christ, and try by every means to make it clear to them, to remove as best we can any difficulties that they may find in it, to impress them with its seriousness, and to urge them to respond to it. This is our abiding responsibility; it is a basic part of our Christian calling.

But now we come to the question that has loomed over us from the outset. How is all this affected by our belief in the sovereignty of God?

We saw earlier that divine sovereignty is one of a pair of truths which form an antinomy in biblical thinking. The God of the Bible is both Lord and Lawgiver in his world; he is both man's King and man's Judge. Consequently, if we would be biblical in our outlook, we have to make room in our minds for the thoughts of divine sovereignty and of human responsibility to stand side by side. Man is indubitably responsible to God, for God is the Lawgiver who fixes his duty, and the Judge who takes account of him as to whether or not he has done it. And God is indubitably sovereign over man, for he controls and orders all human deeds, as he controls and orders all else in his universe. Man's responsibility for his actions, and God's sovereignty in relation to those same actions, are thus, as we saw, equally real and ultimate facts.

The apostle Paul forces this antinomy upon our notice by speaking of God's will (*thelēma*) in connection with both these seemingly incompatible relations of the Creator to his human creatures, and that within the limits of a single short epistle.

In the fifth and sixth chapters of Ephesians, he desires that his readers may "understand what the *will* of the Lord is" (5:17) and "[do] the *will* of God from the heart" (6:6). This is the will of God as Lawgiver, the will of God that man is to know and obey. In the same sense, Paul writes to the Thessalonians: "This is the *will* of God, your sanctification: that you abstain from sexual immorality" (1 Thess 4:3; cf. Mt 7:21; 12:50; Jn 7:17; 1 Jn 2:17, etc.). In the first chapter of Ephesians, however, Paul speaks of God's having chosen him and his fellow Christians in Christ before the world began "according to the purpose of his *will*" (verse 5); he calls God's intention to sum up all things in Christ at the end of the world "the mystery of his *will*" (verse 9); and he speaks of God himself as "him who works all things according to the counsel of his *will*" (verse 11). Here God's "will" is clearly his eternal purpose for the disposal of his creatures, his will as the world's sovereign Lord. This is the will that God actually fulfills in and through everything that actually happens—even man's transgressions of his law.[1] Older theology distinguished the two as God's will of *precept* and his will of *purpose*, the former being his published declaration of what man ought to do, the latter his (largely secret) decision as to what he himself will do. The distinction is between God's *law* and his *plan*. The former tells man what he should be; the latter settles what he will be. Both aspects of the will of God are facts, though how they are related in the mind of God is inscrutable to us. This is one of the reasons why we speak of God as incomprehensible.

---

[1]See, e.g., Gen 1:20; 14:3ff. God's *thelēma* is spoken of in this sense in Rom 1:10; 15:32; Rev 4:11, etc.

Now, our question is: Supposing that all things do in fact happen under the direct dominion of God, and that God has already fixed the future by his decree and resolved whom he will save and whom not—how does this bear on our duty to evangelize?

This is a question that troubles many evangelical Christians today. There are some who have come to believe in the sovereignty of God in the unqualified and uncompromising way in which (as we judge) the Bible presents it. These are now wondering whether there is not some way in which they could and should witness to this faith by modifying the evangelistic practice which they have inherited from a generation with different convictions. These methods, they say, were devised by people who did not believe what we believe about God's absolute sovereignty in salvation; is that not of itself reason enough for refusing to use them? Others, who do not construe the doctrine of divine sovereignty in quite this way, nor take it quite so seriously, fear that this new concern to believe it thoroughly will mean the death of evangelism; for they think it is bound to undercut all sense of urgency in evangelistic action. Satan, of course, will do anything to hold up evangelism and divide Christians; so he tempts the first group to become inhibited and cynical about all current evangelistic endeavors, and the second group to lose its head and become panicky and alarmist, and both to grow self-righteous and bitter and conceited as they criticize each other. Both groups, it seems, have urgent need to watch against the wiles of the devil.

The question, then, is pressing. It was the Bible itself that raised it, by teaching the antinomy of God's dual relation to man; and we look now to the Bible to answer it.

The biblical answer may be stated in two propositions, one negative and one positive.

1. The sovereignty of God in grace does not affect anything that we have said about the nature and duty of evangelism. The principle that operates here is that the rule of our duty and the measure of our responsibility is God's revealed will of precept and not his hidden will of event. We are to order our lives by the light of his law, not by our guesses about his plan. Moses laid down this principle when he had finished teaching Israel the law, the threats and the promises of the Lord. "The secret things belong to the LORD our God, but the things that are revealed belong to us . . . that we may do all the words of this law" (Deut 29:29). The things that God is pleased to keep to himself (the number and identity of the elect, for instance, and when and how he purposes to convert whom) have no bearing on any man's duty. They are not relevant in any way for the interpreting of any part of God's law. Now, the command to evangelize is a part of God's law. It belongs to God's revealed will for his people. It could not, then, in principle be affected in the slightest degree by anything that we might believe about God's sovereignty in election and calling. We may well believe that (in the words of Article XVII of the Church of England) God "hath constantly [i.e., firmly, decisively] decreed by his counsel secret to us, to deliver from curse and damnation those whom he hath chosen in Christ out of mankind, and to bring them by Christ to everlasting salvation, as vessels made to honor." But this does not help us to determine the nature of the evangelistic task, nor does it affect our duty to evangelize universally and indiscriminately. The doctrine of God's sovereignty in grace has no bearing on these things. Therefore we may say:

(1) *The belief that God is sovereign in grace does not affect the* necessity *of evangelism.* Whatever we may believe about election, the fact remains that evangelism is necessary, because no man can be saved without the gospel. "There is no distinction between Jew and Greek," proclaims Paul, "for the same Lord is Lord of all, bestowing his riches on all who call on him. For 'everyone who calls on the name of the Lord [Jesus Christ] will be saved.'" Yes; but nobody will be saved who does not call on the name of the Lord, and certain things must happen before anyone can do this. So Paul continues: "How then shall they call on him in whom they have not *believed?* and how shall they believe in him of whom they have not *heard?* and how shall they hear without a *preacher?*" (Rom 10:14 KJV). They must be told of Christ before they can trust him, and they must trust him before they can be saved by him. Salvation depends on faith, and faith on knowing the gospel. God's way of saving sinners is to bring them to faith through bringing them into contact with the gospel. In God's ordering of things, therefore, evangelism is a necessity if anyone is to be saved at all.

We must realize, therefore, that when God sends us to evangelize, he sends us to act as vital links in the chain of his purpose for the salvation of his elect. The fact that he has such a purpose, and that it is (so we believe) a sovereign purpose that cannot be thwarted, does not imply that, after all, our evangelizing is not needed for its fulfillment. In our Lord's parable, the way in which the wedding was furnished with guests was through the action of the king's servants, who went out as they were bidden into the highways and invited in all whom they found there. Hearing the invitation, the passersby came (Mt 22:1-14). It is in the same way, and through similar action by the servants of God, that the elect come into the salvation that the Redeemer has won for them.

(2) *The belief that God is sovereign in grace does not affect the* urgency *of evangelism.* Whatever we may believe about election, the fact remains that people without Christ are lost, and going to hell (pardon the use of this tarnished phrase: I use it because I mean it). "Unless you repent," said our Lord to the crowd, "you will *all . . . perish*" (Lk 13:3, 5). And we who are Christ's are sent to tell them of the One—the only One—who can save them from perishing. Is not their need urgent? If it is, does that not make evangelism a matter of urgency for us? If you knew that a man was asleep in a blazing building, you would think it a matter of urgency to try and get to him, wake him up and bring him out. The world is full of people who are unaware that they stand under the wrath of God: is it not similarly a matter of urgency that we should go to them, try to arouse them and show them the way of escape?

We should not be held back by the thought that if they are not elect, they will not believe us, and our efforts to convert them will fail. That is true; but it is none of our business and should make no difference to our action. In the first place, it is always wrong to abstain from doing good for fear that it might not be appreciated. In the second place, the nonelect in this world are faceless men as far as we are concerned. We know that they exist, but we do not and cannot know who they are, and it is as futile as it is impious for us to try and guess. The identity of the reprobate is one of God's "secret things" into which his people may not pry. In the third place, our calling as Christians is not to love God's elect, and them only, but to love our neighbor, irrespective of whether he is elect or not. Now, the nature of love is to do good and to relieve need. If, then, our neighbor is unconverted, we are to show love to him as best we can by seeking to share with him the good news without which he will perish. So we find Paul warning and teaching "everyone" (Col 1:28) not merely because he was an apostle, but because every man was his neighbor. And the measure of the urgency of our evangelistic task is the greatness of our neighbor's need and the immediacy of his danger.

(3) *The belief that God is sovereign in grace does not affect the* genuineness *of the gospel invitations, or the* truth *of the gospel promises.* Whatever we may believe about election and, for that matter, about the extent of the atonement, the fact remains that God in the gospel really does offer Christ and promise justification and life to "everyone who calls on the name of the Lord." "Everyone who calls on the name of the Lord will be saved" (Rom 10:13). As God commands all men everywhere to repent, so God invites all men everywhere to come to Christ and find mercy. The invitation is for sinners only, but for sinners universally; it is not for sinners of a certain type only, reformed sinners or sinners whose hearts have been prepared by a fixed minimum of sorrow for sin; but for sinners as such, just as they are. As the hymn puts it:

Let not conscience make you linger,
Nor of fitness fondly dream;

All the fitness He requireth

Is to feel your need of Him.[2]

The fact that the gospel invitation is free and unlimited—"*sinners* Jesus will *receive*," "come *and welcome* to Jesus Christ"[3]—is the glory of the gospel as a revelation of divine grace.

There is a great moment in the holy Communion service of the Church of England when the minister utters the "comfortable words." First the congregation confesses its sins to God in language of extreme strength ("our manifold sins and wickedness . . . provoking most justly thy wrath . . . the burden of them is intolerable. Have mercy upon us, have mercy upon us"). Then the minister turns to face the people and proclaims to them the promises of God.

Hear what comfortable words our Savior Christ said to *all* that truly turn to him:

Come to me, *all* who labor and are heavy laden, and I will give you rest. (Mt 11:28)

God so loved the world, that he gave his only begotten Son, that whosoever believeth in him should not perish, but have everlasting life. (Jn 3:16 KJV)

Hear also what the apostle Paul said:

This is a faithful saying, and worthy of *all* acceptation, that Christ Jesus came into the world to save sinners. (1 Tim 1:15 KJV)

---

[2]From Joseph Hart's "Come, Ye Sinners," *Hymns II* (Downers Grove, Ill.: Inter-Varsity Press, 1976), p. 169. The whole hymn is a magnificent statement of the gospel invitation.

[3]Title of a book by John Bunyan.

Hear also what the apostle John said:

> If *anyone* does sin, we have an advocate with the Father, Jesus Christ the righteous. He is the propitiation for our sins. (1 Jn 2:1-2)

Why are these words "comfortable"? Because they are God's words, and they are all true. They are the essential gospel. They are the promises and assurances which Christians who approach the Lord's Table should come trusting. They are the word which the sacrament confirms. Note them carefully. Note first their *substance*. The object of faith which they present is not mere orthodoxy, not mere truth about Christ's atoning death. It is not less than that, but it is more than that. It is the living Christ himself, the perfect Savior of sinners, who carries in himself all the virtue of his finished work on the cross. "Come *unto me* . . . he is the propitiation for our sins." These promises direct our trust, not to the crucifixion as such, but to Christ crucified; not to his work in the abstract, but to him who wrought it. And note, second, the *universality* of these promises. They offer Christ to *all* who need him, *all* "that truly turn to him," *any man* who has sinned. None are shut out from mercy save those who shut themselves out through impenitence and unbelief.

Some fear that a doctrine of eternal election and reprobation involves the possibility that Christ will not receive some of those who desire to receive him, because they are not elect. The "comfortable words" of the gospel promises, however, absolutely exclude this possibility. As our Lord elsewhere affirmed, in emphatic and categorical terms: "Whoever comes to me I will *never* cast out" (Jn 6:37).

It is true that God has from all eternity chosen whom he will save. It is true that Christ came specifically to save those whom the Father had given him. But it is also true that Christ offers himself freely to all men as their Savior, and guarantees to bring to glory everyone who trusts in him as such. See how he himself deliberately juxtaposes these two thoughts in the following passage:

"I have come down from heaven, not to do my own will but the will of him who sent me. And this is the will of him who sent me, that I should lose nothing of *all that he has given me,* but raise it up on the last day. For this is the will of my Father, that *everyone who looks on the Son and believes in him* should have eternal life, and I will raise him up on the last day" (Jn 6:38-40). "All that he has given me"—here is Christ's saving mission defined in terms of the whole company of the elect, whom he came specifically to save. "Everyone who looks on the Son and believes in him"— here is Christ's saving mission defined in terms of the whole company of lost mankind, to whom he offers himself without distinction and whom he will certainly save if they believe. The two truths stand side by side in these verses, and that is where they belong. They go together. They walk hand in hand. Neither throws doubt on the truth of the other. Neither should fill our minds to the exclusion of the other. Christ means what he says, no less when he undertakes to save all who will trust him than when he undertakes to save all whom the Father has given him.

Thus John Owen, the Puritan, who wrote in defense of both unconditional election and limited atonement, is able—is, indeed, constrained—to address the unconverted as follows:

> Consider the infinite condescension and love of Christ,
> in his invitations and calls of you to come unto him for
> life, deliverance, mercy, grace, peace and eternal salva-
> tion. . . . In the declaration and preaching of them, Jesus
> Christ yet stands before sinners, calling, inviting, en-
> couraging them to come unto him.

> This is somewhat of the word which he now speaks
> unto you: Why will ye die? Why will ye perish? Why
> will ye not have compassion on your own souls? Can
> your hearts endure, or can your hands be strong, in the
> day of wrath that is approaching? . . . Look unto me,
> and be saved; come unto me, and I will ease you of all
> sins, sorrows, fears, burdens, and give rest to your
> souls. Come, I entreat you; lay aside all procrastina-
> tions, all delays; put me off no more; eternity lies at the
> door . . . do not so hate me as that you will rather perish
> than accept of deliverance by me.

> These and the like things doth the Lord Christ con-
> tinually declare, proclaim, plead and urge upon the
> souls of sinners . . . he doth it in the preaching of the
> word, as if he were present with you, stood amongst
> you, and spake personally to every one of you . . . he
> hath appointed the ministers of the gospel to appear
> before you, and to deal with you in his stead, avowing
> as his own the invitations which are given you in his
> name, 2 Corinthians 5:19, 20.[4]

---

[4]John Owen, *The Glory of Christ,* in *The Works of John Owen,* ed. William Goold
(1850), 1:422.

So indeed it is. The invitations of Christ are words of God. They are true. They are meant. They are genuine invitations. They are to be pressed on the unconverted as such. Nothing that we may believe about God's sovereignty in grace makes any difference to this.

(4) *The belief that God is sovereign in grace does not affect* the responsibility of the sinner *for his reaction to the gospel.* Whatever we may believe about election, the fact remains that a man who rejects Christ thereby becomes the cause of his own condemnation. Unbelief in the Bible is a guilty thing, and unbelievers cannot excuse themselves on the grounds that they were not elect. The unbeliever was really offered life in the gospel and could have had it if he would; he, and no one but he, is responsible for the fact that he rejected it, and must now endure the consequences of rejecting it. "Everywhere in Scripture," writes Bishop J. C. Ryle, "it is a leading principle that man can lose his own soul, that if he is lost at last it will be his own fault, and his blood will be on his own head. The same inspired Bible which reveals this doctrine of election is the Bible which contains the words, 'Why will ye die, O house of Israel?'— 'Ye will not come unto me, that ye might have life.'—'This is the condemnation, that light is come into the world, and men loved darkness rather than light, because their deeds were evil' (Ezk 18:31; Jn 5:40, 3:19). The Bible never says that sinners miss heaven because they are not elect, but because they 'neglect the great salvation,' and because they will not repent and believe. The last judgment will abundantly prove that it is not the want of God's election, so

much as laziness, the love of sin, unbelief, and unwilling-
ness to come to Christ, which ruins the souls that are lost."[5]
God gives people what they choose, not the opposite of
what they choose. Those who choose death, therefore, have
only themselves to thank that God does not give them life.
The doctrine of divine sovereignty does not affect the situation in any way.

So much for the first and negative proposition. The second
is positive.

2. *The sovereignty of God in grace gives us our only hope of
success in evangelism.* Some fear that belief in the sovereign
grace of God leads to the conclusion that evangelism is pointless, since God will save his elect anyway, whether they hear
the gospel or not. This, as we have seen, is a false conclusion
based on a false assumption. But now we must go further,
and point out that the truth is just the opposite. So far from
making evangelism pointless, the sovereignty of God in
grace is the one thing that prevents evangelism from being
pointless. For it creates the possibility—indeed, the certainty—that evangelism will be fruitful. Apart from it, there
is not even a possibility of evangelism being fruitful. Were it
not for the sovereign grace of God, evangelism would be the
most futile and useless enterprise that the world has ever
seen, and there would be no more complete waste of time
under the sun than to preach the Christian gospel.

Why is this? Because of the spiritual inability of man in sin.
Let Paul, the greatest of all evangelists, explain this to us:
Fallen man, says Paul, has a blinded mind, and so is unable

---

[5]J. C. Ryle, *Old Paths*, p. 468.

to grasp spiritual truth. "The natural person does not accept the things of the Spirit of God, for they are folly to him, and he is not able to understand them because they are spiritually discerned" (1 Cor 2:14). Again, he has a perverse and ungodly nature. "For the mind that is set on the flesh [the mind of the unregenerate man] is hostile to God, it does not submit to God's law; indeed it cannot." The consequence? "Those who are in the flesh cannot please God" (Rom 8:7-8). In both these passages Paul makes two distinct statements about fallen man in relation to God's truth, and the progression of thought is parallel in both cases. First Paul asserts unregenerate man's failure, as a matter of fact. He "does not accept the things of the Spirit of God"; he "does not submit to God's law." But then Paul goes on to interpret his first statement by a second, to the effect that this failure is a necessity of nature, something certain and inevitable and universal and unalterable, just because it is not in man to do otherwise than fail in this way. "He is *not able* to understand them." "Indeed, it *cannot*." Man in Adam has not got it in him to apprehend spiritual realities or to obey God's law from his heart. Enmity against God, leading to defection from God, is the law of his nature. It is, so to speak, instinctive to him to suppress and evade and deny God's truth, and to shrug off God's authority and to flout God's law—yes, and when he hears the gospel to disbelieve and disobey that too. This is the sort of person that he is. He is, says Paul, "*dead* in the trespasses and sins" (Eph 2:1)—wholly incapacitated for any positive reaction to God's Word, deaf to God's speech, blind to God's revelation, impervious to God's inducements. If you talk to a corpse, there is no response; the man is dead. When God's Word is spoken to sinners, there is equally no response; they are "dead in the trespasses and sins."

Nor is this all. Paul also tells us that Satan (whose power and ill will he never underestimates) is constantly active to keep sinners in their natural state. Satan "is now at work in the sons of disobedience" (Eph 2:2) to ensure that they do not obey God's law. And "the god of this world has blinded the minds of the unbelievers, to keep them from seeing the light of the gospel of the glory of Christ" (2 Cor 4:4). So that there are two obstacles in the way of successful evangelism: the first, man's natural and irresistible impulse to oppose God, and the second, Satan's assiduity in shepherding man in the ways of unbelief and disobedience.

What does this mean for evangelism? It means, quite simply, that evangelism, described as we have described it, cannot possibly succeed. However clear and cogent we may be in presenting the gospel, we have no hope of convincing or converting anyone. Can you or I by our earnest talking break the power of Satan over a man's life? No. Can you or I give life to the spiritually dead? No. Can we hope to convince sinners of the truth of the gospel by patient explanation? No. Can we hope to move men to obey the gospel by any words of entreaty that we may utter? No. Our approach to evangelism is not realistic till we have faced this shattering fact and let it make its proper impact on us. When a schoolmaster is trying to teach children arithmetic or grammar, and finds them slow to learn, he assures himself that the penny must drop sooner or later, and so encourages himself to keep on trying. We can, most of us, muster great reserves of patience if we think that there is some prospect of ultimate success in what we are attempting. But in the case of evangelism there is no such prospect. Regarded as a human enterprise, evangelism is a hopeless task. It cannot in principle produce the desired effect. We can preach, and preach clearly and fluently and attractively; we can talk to individuals in the most pointed and challenging way; we can organize special services and distribute tracts and put up posters and flood the country with publicity—and there is not the slightest prospect that all this outlay of effort will bring a single soul home to God. Unless there is some other factor in the situation, over and above our own endeavors, all evangelistic action is foredoomed to failure. This is the fact, the brute, rock-bottom fact, that we have to face.

Here, I suspect, we find the canker that is really weakening evangelism in evangelical circles today. Everyone seems to agree that our evangelism is not in a healthy state, but there is no agreement as to the nature of the malady or what should be done to cure it. Some, as we have indicated, appear to think that the basic trouble is the current revival in many places of faith in the sovereignty of divine grace—a faith which finds expression in a fresh emphasis on the doctrines of unconditional election and effectual calling. Their remedy, it seems, would be to try and refute, or suppress, these doctrines and to discourage people from taking them seriously. Since, however, so many of the greatest evangelists and missionaries of past days have held precisely these doctrines, it is, to say the least, not obvious that the diagnosis is right, or the suggested remedy appropriate. Moreover, it seems clear that evangelism was languishing between the two world wars, long before this fresh emphasis began to be made. Others, as we have also hinted, appear to locate the trouble in the kind of evangelistic meetings that are commonly held, and they think that if we cut out the jollity and made them more somber, abolishing appeals and counseling rooms and after-meetings, our evangelism would automatically be reinvigorated. But this also is not obvious. I suspect that the root of the trouble with our evangelism today lies deeper than either of these diagnoses goes. I suspect that what is really responsible for this sense of evangelistic malaise is a widespread neurosis of disillusionment, an unacknowledged failure of nerve, springing from a long-standing failure to reckon with the fact that evangelism, regarded as a human enterprise, must be expected to fail. Let me explain.

For about a century now, it has been characteristic of evangelical Christians (rightly or wrongly—we need not discuss that here) to think of evangelism as a specialized activity, best done in short sharp bursts ("missions" or "campaigns"), and needing for its successful practice a distinctive technique, both for preaching and for individual dealing. At an early stage in this period, evangelicals fell into the way of assuming that evangelism was sure to succeed if it was regularly prayed for and correctly run (i.e., if the distinctive technique was used). This was because in those early days, under men like Moody, Torrey, Haslam and Hay Aitken, evangelistic campaigns usually were successful—not because they were always well planned and run (by twenty-first century standards, they often were not), but because God was working in Britain in those days in a way in which he is evidently not working now. Even then, however, it was noticeable that the second mission in any place would rarely be as productive as the first, or the third as the second. But during the past fifty years, as our country has drifted further and further from its Christian moorings, the law of diminishing returns has set in much more drastically. Evangelistic campaigns have become less and less fruitful. And this fact has unnerved us.

Why has it unnerved us? Because we were not prepared for it. We had come to take it for granted that good organization and efficient technique, backed by a routine of prayers, was itself sufficient to guarantee results. We felt that there was an almost magical potency in the special meeting, the special choir and soloist, and the special preacher. We felt convinced that the thing that would always bring life into a dead church, or a dead town, was an intensive evangelistic mission. With the top of our minds, many of us still think that, or profess to think it. We tell each other that it is so and make our plans on this basis. But with the bottom of our minds, in our heart of hearts, we have grown discouraged and disillusioned and apprehensive. Once we thought that well-planned evangelism was sure to succeed, but now we find ourselves afraid each time that it is going to fail, as it has failed so often before. Yet we are afraid to admit our fears to ourselves, for we do not know what to make of a situation in which our planned evangelism fails. So we repress our fears, and our disillusionment becomes a paralyzing neurosis, and our evangelistic practice becomes a jaded and halfhearted routine. Basically, the trouble is our unconfessed doubts as to the worthwhileness of what we are doing.

Why have we these doubts? Because we have been disillusioned. How have we been disillusioned? By the repeated failure of the evangelistic techniques in which we once reposed such confidence. What is the cure of our disillusionment? First, we must admit that we were silly ever to think that any evangelistic technique, however skillful, could of itself guarantee conversions; second, we must recognize that, because man's heart is impervious to the Word of God, it is no cause for surprise if at any time our evangelism fails to result in conversions; third, we must remember that the terms of our calling are that we should be faithful, not that we should be successful; fourth, we must learn to rest all our hopes of fruit in evangelism on the omnipotent grace of God.

For God does what man cannot do. God works by his Spirit through his Word in the hearts of sinful men to bring them to repentance and faith. Faith is a gift of God. "*It has been granted* to you that for the sake of Christ you should . . . believe in him," writes Paul to the Philippians (Phil 1:29). "By grace you have been saved through faith," he tells the Ephesians. "And this is not your own doing; *it is the gift of God*" (Eph 2:8).[6] So, too, repentance is the gift of God. "God exalted him [Christ]," Peter told the Sanhedrin, "as Leader and Savior, to *give* repentance to Israel and forgiveness of sins" (Acts 5:31). When the

---

[6]Whether the gift of God in this text is the act of believing, or the fact of being-saved-through-believing (commentators divide), does not affect our point.

Jerusalem church heard how Peter had been sent to evangelize Cornelius, and how Cornelius had come to faith, they said: "Then to the Gentiles also God has *granted* repentance unto life." You and I cannot make sinners repent and believe in Christ by our words alone; but God works faith and repentance in men's hearts by his Holy Spirit.

Paul terms this God's work of "calling." The old theologians named it "effectual calling," to distinguish it from the ineffective summons that is given when the gospel is preached to a man in whose heart God is not at work. It is the operation whereby God causes sinners to understand and respond to the gospel invitation. It is a work of creative power: by it, God gives men new hearts, freeing them from slavery to sin, abolishing their inability to know and do God's truth, and leading them actually to turn to God and trust Christ as their Savior. By it, also, God breaks Satan's hold on them, delivering them from the domain of darkness and transferring them into "the kingdom of his beloved Son" (Col 1:13). It is thus a calling that creates the response which it seeks, and confers the blessing to which it invites. It is often termed the work of "prevenient grace," because it precedes any motion Godward in the heart of sinful man. It has been described (perhaps misleadingly) as a work of "irresistible grace," simply because it effectively dethrones the disposition to resist grace. The Westminster Confession analyzes it as an activity of God in and on fallen men, "enlightening their minds spiritually and ravingly to understand the things of God; taking away their heart of stone, and giving unto them an heart of flesh; renewing their wills, and by his almighty power determining them to that which is good; and effectually drawing them to Jesus Christ; yet so as they come most freely, being made willing by his grace."[7]

Christ himself taught the universal *necessity* of this calling by the Word and the Spirit. "*No one* can come to me unless the Father who sent me draws him" (Jn 6:44). He also taught the universal *efficacy* of it. "Every one who has heard and learned from the Father comes to me" (Jn 6:45). And with this he taught the universal *certainty* of it for all whom God has chosen. "All that the Father gives me will come to me" (Jn 6:37): they shall hear of me, and they shall be moved to trust me. This is the Father's purpose, and the Son's promise.

Paul speaks of this "effectual calling" as the outworking of God's purpose of election. To the Romans, he says: "Those whom he [God] foreknew he also predestined to be conformed to the image of his Son. . . . And those whom he predestined he also *called,* and those whom he *called* he also justified, and those whom he justified he also glorified" (Rom 8:29-30). To the Thessalonians he writes: "God chose you as the first fruits to be saved, through sanctification by the Spirit and belief in the truth. To this he *called* you through our gospel, so that you may obtain the glory of our Lord Jesus Christ" (2 Thess 2:13-14). The author of the call, the apostle tells us, is God; the mode of calling is by the gospel; and the issue of the call is a title to glory.

But if this is so, then we see at once why it was that Paul, who faced so realistically the fact of fallen man's slavery to sin and Satan, was able to avoid the disillusionment and dis-

---

[7]Westminster Confession, 10:1; cf. Ezek 36:26-27; Jn 6:44-45; 1 Cor 2:10ff.; 2 Cor 4:6; Phil 2:13.

couragement that we feel today as it dawns on us more and more clearly that, humanly speaking, evangelism is a hopeless task. The reason was that Paul kept his eyes firmly fixed on the sovereignty of God in grace. He knew that God had long before declared that "my word . . . that goes out from my mouth; / it shall not return to me empty, / but it shall accomplish that which I purpose, / and shall succeed in the thing for which I sent it" (Is 55:11). He knew that this was no less true of the gospel than of any other divine utterance. He knew, therefore, that his own preaching of the gospel would not, in the long run, prove fruitless. God would see to that. He knew that wherever the word of the gospel went, God would raise the dead. He knew that the word would prove a savior of life to some of those who heard it. This knowledge made him confident, tireless and expectant in his evangelism. And if there were on occasion hard spells, with much opposition and little visible fruit, he did not panic or lose heart. For he knew that if Christ had opened the door for him to make known the gospel in a place, that meant that it was Christ's purpose to draw sinners to himself in that place. The word would not return void. His business, therefore, was to be patient and faithful in spreading the good news till the time of harvest should come.

There was a time at Corinth when things were hard; there had been some converts, certainly, but opposition was mounting and even Paul, the dauntless, was wondering whether it was worth persevering there. "And," we are told, "the Lord [Jesus] said to Paul one night in a vision, 'Do not be afraid, but go on speaking and do not be silent, for I am with you, and no one will attack you to harm you, *for I have many in this city who are my people*'" (Acts 18:9-10). As if to say: go on preaching and teaching, Paul, and let nothing stop you; there are many here whom I mean to bring to myself through your testimony to my gospel. "This confirms St. Luke's emphasis upon the prevenient choice of God," comments Richard B. Rackham.[8] And Luke's emphasis reflects Paul's conviction, based on Christ's own assurance to him. Thus the sovereignty of God in grace gave Paul hope of success as he preached to deaf ears, and held up Christ before blind eyes, and sought to move stony hearts. His confidence was that where Christ sends the gospel there Christ has his people—fast bound at present in the chains of sin, but due for release at the appointed moment through a mighty renewing of their hearts as the light of the gospel shines into their darkness and the Savior draws them to himself.

In a great hymn that he wrote shortly after his conversion (possibly the day after), Charles Wesley spoke of what had happened like this:

> Long my imprisoned spirit lay
> Fast bound in sin and nature's night;
> Thine eye diffused a quickening ray,—
> I woke, the dungeon flamed with light;
> My chains fell off, my heart was free,
> I rose, went forth, and followed thee.[9]

That is not only a vivid statement of experience; it is also a

---

[8]*The Acts of the Apostles*, p. 327; cf. Acts 13:48.
[9]From "And Can It Be," *Hymns II* (Downers Grove, Ill.: InterVarsity Press, 1976), p. 88.

piece of excellent theology. This is precisely what happens to unconverted men and women wherever the gospel is preached. Paul knew that; hence his confidence and expectancy when evangelizing.

Paul's confidence should be our confidence too. We may not trust in our methods of personal dealing or running evangelistic services, however excellent we may think them. There is no magic in methods, not even in theologically impeccable methods. When we evangelize, our trust must be in God who raises the dead. He is the almighty Lord who turns people's hearts, and he will give conversions in his own time. Meanwhile, our part is to be faithful in making the gospel known, sure that such labor will never be in vain. This is how the truth of the sovereignty of God's grace bears on evangelism.

What effects should this confidence and certainty have on our attitude when evangelizing? Three at least.

(1) *It should make us bold.* It should keep us from being daunted when we find, as we often do, that people's first reaction to the gospel is to shrug it off in apathy or even contempt. Such a reaction should not surprise us; it is only to be expected from the bondslaves of sin and Satan. Nor should it discourage us; for no heart is too hard for the grace of God. Paul was a bitter opponent of the gospel, but Christ laid his hand on Paul, and Paul was broken down and born again. You yourself, since you became a Christian, have been learning constantly how corrupt and deceitful and perverse your own heart is; before you became a Christian, your heart was worse; yet Christ has saved you, and that should be enough to convince you that he can save anyone. So persevere in

presenting Christ to unconverted people as you find opportunity. You are not on a fool's errand. You are not wasting either your time or theirs. You have no reason to be ashamed of your message, or halfhearted and apologetic in delivering it. You have every reason to be bold, and free, and natural, and hopeful of success. For God can give his truth an effectiveness that you and I cannot give it. God can make his truth triumphant to the conversion of the most seemingly hardened unbeliever. You and I will never write off anyone as hopeless and beyond the reach of God if we believe in the sovereignty of his grace.

(2) *This confidence should make us patient.* It should keep us from being daunted when we find that our evangelistic endeavors meet with no immediate response. God saves in his own time, and we ought not to suppose that he is in such a hurry as we are. We need to remember that we are all children of our age, and the spirit of our age is a spirit of tearing hurry. And it is a pragmatic spirit; it is a spirit that demands quick results. The modern ideal is to achieve more and more by doing less and less. This is the age of the labor-saving device, the efficiency chart and automation. The attitude that all this breeds is one of impatience toward everything that takes time and demands sustained effort. Ours tends to be a slapdash age; we resent spending time doing things thoroughly. This spirit tends to infect our evangelism (not to speak of other departments of our Christianity), and with disastrous results. We are tempted to be in a great hurry with those whom we would win to Christ, and then, when we see no immediate response in them, to become impatient and downcast, and

then to lose interest in them and feel that it is useless to spend more time on them; so we abandon our efforts forthwith and let them drop out of our ken. But this is utterly wrong. It is a failure both of love for people and of faith in God.

The truth is that the work of evangelizing demands more patience and sheer "stickability," more reserves of persevering love and care, than most of us twenty-first-century Christians have at command. It is a work in which quick results are not promised; it is a work, therefore, in which the non-appearance of quick results is no sign of failure; but it is a work in which we cannot hope for success unless we are prepared to persevere with people. The idea that a single evangelistic sermon, or a single serious conversation, ought to suffice for the conversion of anyone who is ever going to be converted is really silly. If you see someone whom you meet come to faith through a single such sermon or talk, you will normally find that his heart was already well prepared by a good deal of Christian teaching and exercise of spirit prior to your meeting with him. The law that operates in such cases is "one sows and another reaps" (Jn 4:37). If, on the other hand, you meet a person who is not thus prepared, a person who as yet has no conviction of the truth of the gospel and perhaps no idea, or even a false idea, of what the gospel actually is, it is worse than useless to try and stampede him into a snap "decision." You may be able to bully him into a psychological crisis of some sort, but that will not be saving faith and will do him no good. What you have to do is to take time with him, to make friends with him, to get alongside him, to find out where he is in terms of spiritual understanding, and to start dealing with him at that point. You have to explain the gospel to him, and be sure that he understands it and is convinced of its truth, before you start pressing him to an active response. You have to be ready to help him, if need be, through a spell of seeking to repent and believe before he knows within himself that he has received Christ, and Christ has received him. At each stage you have to be willing to go along with him at God's speed, which may seem to you a strangely slow speed. But that is God's business, not yours. Your business is simply to keep pace with what God is doing in his life. Your willingness to be patient with him in this way is the proof of your love of him no less than of your faith in God. If you are not willing thus to be patient, you need not expect that God will favor you by enabling you to win souls.

Where does the patience come from that is so indispensable for evangelistic work? From dwelling on the fact that God is sovereign in grace and that his word does not return to him void; that it is he who gives us such opportunities as we find for sharing our knowledge of Christ with others, and that he is able in his own good time to enlighten them and bring them to faith. God often exercises our patience in this, as in other matters. As he kept Abraham waiting twenty-five years for the birth of his son, so he often keeps Christians waiting for things that they long to see, such as the conversion of their friends. We need patience, then, if we are to do our part in helping others toward faith. And the way for us to develop that patience is to learn to live in terms of our knowledge of the free and gracious sovereignty of God.

(3) *Finally, this confidence should make us prayerful.* Prayer,

as we said at the beginning, is a confessing of impotence and need, an acknowledging of help, lessness and dependence, and an invoking of the mighty power of God to do for us what we cannot do for ourselves. In evangelism, as we saw, we are impotent; we depend wholly on God to make our witness effective; only because he is able to give men new hearts can we hope that through our preaching of the gospel sinners will be born again. These facts ought to drive us to prayer. It is God's intention that they should drive us to prayer. God means us, in this as in other things, to recognize and confess our impotence, and to tell him that we rely on him alone, and to plead with him to glorify his name. It is his way regularly to withhold his blessings until his people start to pray. "You do not have, because you do not ask" (Jas 4:2). "Ask, and it will be given to you; seek, and you will find; knock, and it will be opened to you" (Mt 7:7). But if you and I are too proud or lazy to ask, we need not expect to receive. This is the universal rule, in evangelism as elsewhere. God will make us pray before he blesses our labors in order that we may constantly learn afresh that we depend on God for everything. And then, when God permits us to see conversions, we shall not be tempted to ascribe them to our own gifts, or skill, or wisdom, or persuasiveness, but to his work alone, and so we shall know whom we ought to thank for them.

The knowledge, then, that God is sovereign in grace, and that we are impotent to win souls, should make us pray and keep us praying. What should be the burden of our prayers? We should pray for those whom we seek to win, that the Holy Spirit will open their hearts; and we should pray for ourselves in our own witness, and for all who preach the gospel, that the power and authority of the Holy Spirit may rest on them. "Pray for us," writes Paul to the Thessalonians, "that the word of the Lord may speed ahead and be honored" (2 Thess 3:1). Paul was a great evangelist who had seen much fruit, but Paul knew that every particle of it had come from God, and that unless God continued to work both in him and in those to whom he preached he would never convert another soul. So he pleads for prayer, that his evangelism might still prove fruitful. Pray, he pleads, that the word of the gospel may be glorified through my preaching of it, and through its effect in human lives. Pray that it may be used constantly to the conversion of sinners. This, to Paul, is an urgent request, just because Paul sees so clearly that his preaching can save nobody unless God in sovereign mercy is pleased to bless it and use it to this end. Paul, you see, does not hold that, because God is sovereign in saving sinners, therefore prayer is needless, any more than he holds that, because God is sovereign in saving sinners, evangelistic preaching is needless. Rather, he holds that, just because the salvation of sinners depends wholly on God, prayer for the fruitfulness of evangelistic preaching is all the more necessary. And those today who, with Paul, believe most strongly that it is the sovereign agency of God—and that alone—that leads sinners to Christ should bear witness to their faith by showing themselves most constant and faithful and earnest and persistent in prayer that God's blessing may rest on the preaching of his Word, and that under it sinners may be born again. This is the final bearing of belief in the sovereignty of God's grace on evangelism.

We said earlier in this chapter that this doctrine does not in any way reduce or narrow the terms of our evangelistic commission. Now we see that, so far from contracting them, it actually expands them. For it faces us with the fact that there are two sides to the evangelistic commission. It is a commission not only to preach but also to pray; not only to talk to men about God, but also to talk to God about men. Preaching and prayer must go together; our evangelism will not be according to knowledge, nor will it be blessed, unless they do. We are to preach, because without knowledge of the gospel no man can be saved. We are to pray, because only the sovereign Holy Spirit in us and in men's hearts can make our preaching effective to men's salvation, and God will not send his Spirit where there is no prayer. Evangelicals are at present busy reforming their methods of evangelistic preaching, and that is good. But it will not lead to evangelistic fruitfulness unless God also reforms our praying, and pours out on us a new spirit of supplication for evangelistic work. The way ahead for us in evangelism is that we should be taught afresh to testify to our Lord and to his gospel, in public and in private, in preaching and in personal dealing, with boldness, patience, power, authority and love; and that with this we should also be taught afresh to pray for God's blessing on our witness with humility and importunity. It is as simple—and as difficult—as that. When all has been said that has to be said about the reformation of evangelistic methods, it still remains that there is no way ahead but this, and if we do not find this way, we will not advance.

Thus the wheel of our argument comes full circle. We began by appealing to our practice of prayer as proof of our faith in divine sovereignty. We end by applying our faith in divine sovereignty as a motive to the practice of prayer.

What, then, are we to say about the suggestion that a hearty faith in the absolute sovereignty of God is inimical to evangelism? We are bound to say that anyone who makes this suggestion thereby shows that he has simply failed to understand what the doctrine of divine sovereignty means. Not only does it undergird evangelism, and uphold the evangelist, by creating a hope of success that could not otherwise be entertained; it also teaches us to bind together preaching and prayer; and as it makes us bold and confident before men, so it makes us humble and importunate before God. Isn't this as it should be? We would not wish to say that man cannot evangelize at all without coming to terms with this doctrine; but we venture to think that, other things being equal, he will be able to evangelize better for believing it.